The
Tucker - Tyler
Adventure

Happy trails!

Love,

The
Tucker ~ Tyler
Adventure

By

Katherine Tucker and Marialyce Tyler

with

Nancy Cowan and Tara Taft

Bootjack Press, P.O. Box 305, Stow, Mass. 01775

Cover design and maps by Betsy Stepp

Photographs by Katherine Tucker and Marialyce Tyler

ISBN: 978-0-9914826-0-3

This book is available from Amazon.com and other bookstores

This book is dedicated to our moms and their adventurous spirits and to the adventures of their grandchildren and great-grandchildren in the years to come.

Oct. 31, 1954   6957

PARIS
LA TOUR EIFFEL
SOMMET 300 MÈTRES

31 X 54 — PARIS VII

RÉPUBLIQUE
FRANÇAISE
1800
POSTES

SOUVENIR DE LA TOUR EIFFEL

Hi!
Paris is wonderful!
The most beautiful
view imaginable —
Were at the tower very
day!! Someday —
Paris is more exciting
than ever — Wish you
were here
Marianne

Mrs. Alice Tyler
Fort Pierre
South Dakota
U.S.A.

80 — PARIS - La Tour Eiffel.
Construite de 1887 à 1889. Hauteur:
300 m. Poids: 7 millions de kilos. Distance d'axe en axe des piliers: 104 m.
2.500.000 rivets relient ses 15.000 pièces
de métal. La 1re plate-forme est à 57 m.
La 2e à 115 m. La 3e à 280 m. Les esca-
liers comportent 1.710 marches.

Édition spéciale de la TOUR EIFFEL
PHOTO VÉRITABLE

I just can't put down everything I want to – Hope these tiny dull notes will help me to sketch the picture so that years from now when I read it I will be able to fill in the details.

~Kit Tucker

Table of Contents

Preface

"What was it like to be on the *Queen Mary*?" I asked Marialyce (Rusty) Tyler Dorward, 50 years after she and her friend, Katherine (Kit) Tucker Cowan sailed to Europe. "It's all in my letters," she replied. Letters? What letters? Moments later, she handed me a box of letters handwritten on airmail stationery. In 1954, Marialyce, my mother, wrote over 35 letters from Europe home to her mother, Alice Tyler, in Fort Pierre, South Dakota.

I read letters out loud to Mom and Kit when we visited on Martha's Vineyard a year later. The two laughed while reminiscing; I listened and took notes of more stories and learned that Kit still had her letters as well. Kit sent 26 letters and postcards home to her family in New Jersey. Both women had saved all their slides, Kit had her journal (Rusty's was stolen on the trip). Both still had the postcards they sent home.

In the following pages, Kit's daughter, Nancy Cowan, and I have attempted to compile the best of the letters, Kit's journal, their postcards and the slides, presenting *The Tucker-Tyler Adventure*, a glimpse into the lives of two young women and the 1954 world in which they traveled.

—Tara Taft

Introduction

Imagine the world without the Internet, when a cup of coffee costs only five cents and a woman's purse and hat match her shoes. Imagine a world brought to you only through the movies or books, radio broadcasts or the newsreel; the widespread viewing of television is just beginning. If you want to make a telephone call, you have to dial the number on a telephone connected to the wall, and if no one is home, there is no way to leave a message. Long distance calls are expensive, and international calls are only for the very rich.

In 1954, the Korean War has just ended, and World War II remains a recent memory. The U.S., Great Britain, and France are still occupying the western portion of Germany. McCarthy is just beginning to hold hearings on alleged Communism in the Army, and the Baby Boom is at its height.

After years of scrimping, the 1950s are a prosperous time for Americans whose average annual income is $2,992. A typical American spends $85 a month on rent, 22 cents a gallon for gas, and 70 cents to watch movies such as *An American in Paris* and *Roman Holiday*. In New York, Ellis Island closes to immigrants, *The Nutcracker* is staged for the first time, and *The Tonight Show* is first aired with Steve Allen as host. Popular songs include "That's Amore" by Dean Martin, "Three Coins in the Fountain" by the Four Aces, "Rock Around the Clock" by Bill Haley and the Comets, and "Sh-Boom" by the Crew Cuts.

Although 33 percent of American women work in 1950, many women feel pressured to marry right out of high school or college and become housewives. The number of women attending college declines, and women call themselves "girls," no matter what their age.

In 1954, two young women, a country girl and a city girl, both just a few years out of college and ready for adventure, board the RMS *Queen Mary* and forge into a world unknown to them.

From September 8, 1954 until December 16, 1954, Marialyce (Rusty) Tyler and Katherine (Kit) Tucker travel by ship, train, ferry, and car throughout Europe, visiting 13 countries and staying in 42 cities. On little more, and sometimes less, than $5 a day, they stay in hotels, B&Bs, and private homes, meet Americans and Europeans, tour museums, and eat the local cuisine.

Although both women (or "girls" as they call themselves) go by various names, (Katherine, Bootie, Butch, and Kit; Marialyce, Tam, and Rusty), we've chosen to refer to them by the names with which they referred to each other: Kit and Rusty.

It all begins in New York City where Kit and Rusty first meet.

The Queen Mary docking – April 1954 from window in Room 2806. RKO Building. NYC. – Rusty

NEW YORK

Last night, as I stood in the bow and looked back up at the wide, sweeping bridge where the Captain or officer of the watch stands, I realized what an exciting and important step Rusty and I had taken. It is truly unbelievable!

~Kit Tucker

1

Meeting the Girls (1928 – 1954)

The City Girl

Katherine always knew she would move to New York City. "When you grew up in New Jersey," Katherine said, "It was the logical place to go to work. My dad commuted to New York for years so I knew it pretty well, and I loved it."

Less than 15 miles from New York City, Katherine Tucker was born on July 19, 1928, to parents Philip and Katherine Tucker. The younger of two children, Katherine was raised with her sister, Helen, in East Orange, New Jersey, where the population was 68,028 in 1930.

Known to her friends in East Orange as "Bootie" (a nickname given by her sister), Katherine graduated from East Orange's Upsala College in 1950, with a double major in English and psychology and a minor in geology. By the time she graduated, Katherine was ready to move to the Big City.

A friend of Katherine's found her an interview at NBC. She was hired on the spot and began working in NBC's personnel department as a secretary, performing all stenographic functions, handling phone calls, maintaining placement files, administering aptitude and clerical tests, and screening walk-in applicants.

But Katherine wouldn't be Katherine for long. Telling her that "Bootie" wouldn't do when asked if she had a nickname, her new boss, placement manager of the personnel department, assigned her the nickname, "Kit."

According to Kit, her first apartment in New York City was "an awful place to live." The building was located right next to the holding pens for cattle going to slaughter. Kit said the cows used to moo all night long, right under her window. She and her roommate, a friend from college, stayed less than a month before finding another flat, "a neat place up on East 75th Street."

At that time, many apartments came furnished, so moving from one to the other required nothing more than packing a few suitcases and calling a cab. Kit lived in several apartments over the next four years, on the East and the West Sides, until her last apartment on East 84th Street. This railroad flat, an apartment with a series of rooms connected by a long hall and little ventilation, would get hot, making it difficult to sleep. During the middle of the night, people from the apartment building would walk over to the river for the breeze.

Back at the office, Kit made many friends in the personnel department. Once a week, a group would go to one of the little French restaurants on the West Side and eat lunch for 99 cents. According to Kit, the price was 99 cents because once the price reached $1 the restaurant would have to charge tax. After work, everyone headed out for drinks to a small bar next to Rockefeller Center named Hurley's. If it was a special occasion, such as a birthday or a good-bye party, they went up to the Rainbow Room on the 65th floor of 30 Rockefeller Center (known as the RCA Building at the time) to celebrate.

After 2½ years in personnel, "It got boring," Kit said. In February 1953, she was transferred to the local radio/TV station where they called her a program assistant, "But I was just a secretary," she said. As executive secretary and operations assistant to the WRCA program manager, she continued with her secretarial duties and assisted with special projects for the program manager as well. Down the hall from Kit's desk, Barbara Walters worked as secretary to NBC's station manager.

Kit loved music and the arts. While working at NBC, she attended many rehearsals and performances. At one point, she had the job of distributing extra tickets for the NBC Orchestra which Arturo Toscanini conducted. She went to the ballet and the opera, climbing five flights of stairs for the Family Circle standing-room-only seats. Kit loved to sing and became a member of the Rockefeller Center Chorus, which performed under the large tree every year at Christmas time.

Kit was working for the program manager of the local NBC radio station affiliate when Marialyce, a red-headed girl, showed up to occupy the desk next to her that had been empty for several months. According to Kit, Marialyce already had a big group of friends from her theater pursuits and also from being a Guidette at NBC.

The Country Girl

As an only child living on a ranch in Fort Pierre, South Dakota, Marialyce Tyler grew up pretending and imagining. Born on Christmas Day in 1929, Marialyce lived her first few years in the city of Bismarck, North Dakota. When she was five years old, her parents, Alice Schomer Tyler and James Wilbur Tyler, separated, and she and her mother moved back to the family ranch in Fort Pierre. Marialyce heard stories from her grandparents and uncles and listened while her mother read to her from *Richard Halliburton's Complete Book of Marvels*, a book which, with its descriptions of cities, mountains, and temples, instilled in Marialyce a sense of adventure and curiosity for other lands and other people.

After experiencing the thrill of being on stage while a student at Fort Pierre High School, Marialyce knew she wanted to be an actress. She attended Yankton College in Yankton, South Dakota, for two years before transferring to Northwestern University near Chicago. From September 1950 to June 1952, she studied under Alvina Krauss at Northwestern's School of Speech. Mrs. Krause taught Marialyce how to speak without a South Dakota accent, among other theatrical lessons, and by the time she graduated, Marialyce was ready to move to New York City.

Accompanied by her college friends, Evelyn Luft from New Jersey and Billie Ann Couch from Louisiana, the South Dakota girl arrived in the Big City in early September 1952 and moved into an apartment at 40 West 74th Street. Just a short walk to Central Park West, the apartment was the old library of a brownstone they called the "Borden Mansion." According to Rusty, "We were on the first floor, a 14-foot ceilinged room with a huge marble fireplace, tall windows draped in dark red velvet and then beyond a huge room that had three twin-sized beds, a very large and long dark mahogany dining table, chairs, etc., a small one-person-at-a-time kitchen, and beyond that a bathroom that had been made out of a closet." Soon after, another college classmate, Tish Pierce from Michigan, moved in, and the apartment's rent of $140 was divided between them.

All dressed up, in matching hats and shoes, Marialyce, Evelyn, and Billie Ann went to an employment office. "We asked, 'How do we get a job? What can we do?' The man [in the office] looked at us, turned around in his seat (trying not to laugh), got out his phone and called NBC," Marialyce said. "We went to NBC to become Guidettes." It was at NBC where someone nicknamed Marialyce "Rusty" for her deep reddish rust-colored hair. The name stuck and throughout her time in New York, she was called Rusty by everyone except her college friends who still called her Marialyce.

As an NBC Guidette, Rusty went through training to learn how to take people through the studios and show them how NBC worked. "We had a 'patter' – a big long thing we had to memorize," she said.

Wearing a navy blue skirt, a light blue blazer with epaulettes, and pumps, Rusty took people through the rooms at NBC Studios, showing them where their favorite shows were produced and how some of the sound effects they heard on the radio were created. "We had all sorts of sound effects we used," Rusty said. "We'd show them how to make the noises of horses clomping."

On September 16, 1952, Rusty, Evelyn, and Billie Ann had their first "At Home" at 40 West 74th Street. After work on Tuesday nights, they entertained friends with weekly parties they called "At Homes." The girls provided the place and the coffee. The parties were casual and open to any of their friends. They never knew how many people would show up. Evelyn said years later, "We asked people to bring some friends and refreshment. We met interesting people and ate interesting food." When Billie Ann married in June, the others moved to an apartment on West 121st Street, and by January, they were living in an apartment owned by a friend of Evelyn's at 68 West 68th Street.

Whatever her job as Guidette paid, it wasn't enough. Rusty wrote to a friend in January 1953 that she had no money:

> I have only thirty some dollars in the bank […] I'm so flat broke now – have 25 cents to last till pay-day – on Thursday!! So am going to have to borrow again – this is really awful! But you never know, - maybe this spring I can make it … keep your fingers crossed! —Rusty

Eventually, Rusty gave up her job as Guidette and began working on some of the NBC productions. It was then that she met Kit. Rusty was script girl, program assistant, and assistant director for several TV and radio shows, including *Firestone Hour*, *Your Hit Parade*, and *Three Steps to Heaven*. Her salary in April 1953 was $210 per month. "I can't remember the names of all the shows," she said. "On one show, I sat at a table with a man in a big huge room. We were on the air, and he was singing to me. (I was just listening.) That was fun."

Another time, Rusty worked on a new radio quiz show, *The Baron and the Bee*, which Jack Pearl and Cliff "Sharley" Hall were trying to sell as a package to NBC. She wrote to a friend,

> *So I played one of the contestants – was paid $15.00 for it – I had all of about three – no, four, lines. But it was a spelling bee … and I was always the last woman up and battling back and forth with the last man on the other team (in rehearsal, that is, and the two tapings of the show). They had it in 6A – large studio! And with a packed audience; who of course when given tickets on the Mezzanine didn't realize that it wasn't going to be on the air until after they were seated. But they enjoyed it. … The show got terrific response. Am anxious to see if NBC will buy it! —Rusty*

When Steve Allen started the *Tonight Show*, NBC did a lot to promote the new show. One day, all the secretaries (including Kit and Rusty) were rounded up to do publicity shots with Allen. Another time, Kit had a bit part on the show. According to Kit, Allen was nice, but it wasn't fun to be alone with Gene Rayburn, the original announcer for the show, who was constantly chasing all the young women at NBC.

Three Steps to Heaven was a soap opera that began airing on TV on August 3, 1953. "I had a stool and a watch clock that I used to time the show. I would lead all the rehearsals, and when it went on the air, I was supposed to be the one to time it." But when it actually did air, the company brought in a man to do the job, "'Because,' they told me, 'Women couldn't do that.'"

"He [her replacement] sat on my stool!" she said. "I took it for

Fort Pierre Girl To Tour Europe

Miss Maryalyce Tyler of Ft. Pierre has completed arrangements for her European trip and will sail on the Queen Mary from New York on September 8, docking at Cherbourg and going directly to Paris.

Miss Tyler, who has been spending the summer with her mother Mrs. Alice Tyler, will leave Ft. Pierre next week to attend a wedding in New York before sailing.

With Miss Kit Tucker, Miss Tyler will tour several European countries before they go to Rome where they will work and study.

Miss Tyler, following graduation from Ft. Pierer high school, tion from Ft. Pierre high school, attended Yankton College and Northwestern University where she received her degree in speech with a major in theater. She has had stage and TV experience in New York.

awhile. I went in to see the gal who'd given me the job, and I said, 'This is stupid. I've had enough. I want to do more.' She said, 'As a woman there's nothing more you can do. I know it's not right, but …' I said, 'In that case, I'm quitting.'"

"I walked downstairs. Kit and I sat next to each other (our desks were side by side)," Rusty said.

"I'll never forget how it happened," Kit said. "She was rummaging in her file drawer next to my typewriter. She looked up at me and said, 'Kit, have you ever thought about going to Europe?' I said, 'You bet,' and that was it." Almost a year later, on September 8, 1954, Rusty Tyler joined Kit Cowan, embarking on the RMS *Queen Mary* and beginning what they later called, "The Tucker – Tyler Adventure."

The Queen Mary

It's the strangest feeling to look ahead and see
this huge ship forging ahead to — where?
It's all so "unknown."

~Rusty Tyler

2

Sailing to Europe
(September 8 – September 13, 1954)

Almost 20 years after her maiden voyage on May 27, 1936, two young women boarded the RMS *Queen Mary* and headed to Europe – no *Let's Go* travel guide in their hands, no Eurail Pass, no backpacks, and no phones. The voyage took five days and, based on letters the girls wrote, was a non-stop party. It was a grand beginning to a grand trip, and Rusty captured the excitement when she wrote home:

> It *really* *must* *be* *true*. Kit and I just came down from the
> Promenade – the wind nearly blew us off!! – (overboard, that is!)
> The moon is shining a bit behind clouds – and there's inky black
> water everywhere! What a foamy white froth we're turning up as
> we plow through. – It's the strangest feeling to look ahead and see
> this huge ship forging ahead to — where? It's all so "unknown."
> —Rusty

The first order of business for the girls was to find their cabin and settle in. Kit wrote the details in her journal:

Arrived at ship R.M.S. Queen Mary at approximately 11:00 a.m. this morning. Stateroom number is 211 on A Deck. Our cabin is very nice – we are very lucky to be in such a good spot since there are 3 decks of Tourist Class beneath us where cabins are smaller. We have double decker bunks, 2 chairs, 2 closets, chest and sink. —Kit

Built in the early 1930s as an ocean liner for the British-owned Cunard Line, the RMS *Queen Mary* was tall and long. From her keel to her smokestack, she stood 181 feet high, and at 1,019.5 feet, she was almost as long as the Eiffel Tower was tall. She could carry as many as 1,957 passengers on her 12 decks. She was sophisticated too, with her art deco interior design a signature of the era. She sailed primarily from England to the United States and was used for troop transport during World War II.

Kit mentioned "Tourist Class" in the journal entry above with little sense of interest in it. Rusty sounded a bit more intrigued by the class distinctions when she wrote home to her mother that they "discovered that the 3 classes are very definitely separated! There are locked gates dividing the halls, etc. We shall never see or know who is traveling 1st or cabin class – It is impossible, there are 3 of everything: movies, dining rooms, etc."

Rusty underestimated their resourcefulness and their social skills. The girls, and the friends they made on the boat, found their way into Cabin and First Class several times during the voyage. Kit said that someone tipped them off regarding the secret way to First Class – go down a certain number of levels and then walk through the kitchens until you get to the passageway for First Class. "Nobody bothers you!" she was told. They made several forays to First Class and Cabin Class – a few times to swim and a few times to dance but tried not to overdo it lest they be noticed.

Rusty and Kit's cabin was the site of the first of many parties they would attend on the *Queen Mary*. Approximately 30 people came to see them off on September 8 bearing all kinds of gifts – including candy, corsages, and telegrams. Kit later mentioned that she was particularly amazed by the presence of one guest, her cousin Virginia. Virginia said she saw the announcement of Kit's trip in the newspaper and decided to show up as a surprise.

Rusty described the scene in their cabin:

> *Over 30 people came to see us off!!! Bob Spinok brought me a box of candy; Art Topal and Mary Baker brought a huge box of candy too and several very numerous appropriate "items" – Milt (best man at Eve's and Cal's wedding) sent me a book, — Greg and Billie sent us each a corsage of roses; — And I received 3 telegrams from Tami, Arnie, and Cal and Evelyn. Then Kit rec'd many things, too, — including 2 large bouquets of flowers! — You should see our room now!!!* —Rusty

The partygoers were asked to leave the ship by 1:30 p.m., and Kit later wrote to her parents:

> *After you left, we wandered around the ship for awhile ending up in our cabin – what a mess! Daddy, you talk about Jim Davis' bar – well – Jim's has nothing on us – we even found champagne running around in one of the bureau drawers! It will probably take several days for the aroma to work its way out.* —Kit

*After the party! Aboard the Queen Mary Cabin #221-A.
– Rusty*

At 2:45 p.m. on September 8, 1954, Kit and Rusty stood at the rail of the ship, in the rain, waving goodbye to their family, friends, and country. Rusty wrote home, "People were waving and yelling goodbye, and I got the <u>funniest</u> feeling when I saw a little girl waving an American flag – Then we turned and started down the Hudson on 'our' own power."

Rusty and Kit began unpacking, exploring, and eating. Kit wrote home that at dinner that night they ate "Roast beef, string beans, potatoes and Yorkshire pudding ... but it wasn't half as good as Hampshire House last night with exactly the same thing. The British certainly <u>do</u> cook their meat to death!"

The first day also brought a first new friend, as Kit described in a letter home:

> *Pops, the flowers are simply beautiful! Thank you ever so much – we were sitting there admiring them – with the door open for air when a terribly British voice said "What lovely flowers!" and standing in the doorway was a partly balding gentleman, dressed in clerical garb – sporting gray trousers, a black jacket, a scarlet tunic and a long silver chain with a silver cross around his neck and a white clerical collar ... he is the Right Reverend I.S. Watkins, Bishop of Malmesbury, England. What a darling he is! Every time he goes down the corridor, he stops to chat – loves to talk. He has given us all sorts of "fatherly" advice (he has a daughter named May – just about our age). He is really the epitome of an Anglican country type Bishop from a story book. He'll tell stories by the hour – he came in "just for a moment" on his way to dinner and stayed a half hour – doing all the talking – told two jokes which I think I remember from my grammar school days and enjoyed them tremendously – Rusty and I laughed gaily and after he left, compared notes – she had heard them years ago too – very British.*
> —Kit

A couple of weeks later, Rusty wrote home about a "best friend" she had brought along in her suitcase.

> *Oh yes, and I wanted to tell you – I love my trench coat, and have worn it soooo much already! Between now and sunny (?) Italy, I*

think I shall be living in it! A man on the Queen Mary told me as we passed on a staircase, — "Don't ever part with that coat, — it will be your best friend from now on" — And I believe him!
—Rusty

The first night on board there was a "Get Together Dance" held in the Smoke Room. The girls got off to a quick start forming a group of friends, some of whom they would encounter again later in their travels. Kit described the dance in her journal:

Started out to be a real bomb with dance games etc. but about 11:30 young Britisher asked me to dance and brought with him a friend who wanted to meet us — things progressed from there and we ended up at 4:00 am. First young man's name is Tony and he looks like a character in the "Pickwick Papers" – pink cheeks and his hair! He is balding down the middle with bunches of hair on either side which are long and curly and brushed up to form little poufs over his ears. He is very English and very funny. —Kit

Rusty provided the juicier bit when she wrote home to her mother "I sort of ended up with Chris and Kit with Tony."

The cast of characters on the boat is described in detail by Rusty in a letter home dated September 15. She began by describing Tony:

He was very sweet and very funny! ... He majored in International Affairs at Oxford University and came to the University of Virginia to write his thesis on America's Foreign Diplomacy; Kit said she thought that was a hard place to find out what it is. Tony replied that Oh yes! He had discovered it all right. We asked, "What is it?" And he said, "They haven't any!" Which we laughed at and thought, "Mmm, that's about right." —Rusty

Rusty followed this description of Tony with a list of all the people to whom Tony introduced them:

Chris Willy – smooth, very good looking, an "operator" — and most entertaining! He also attended Oxford University; and during the summers, he took <u>tours</u> of American women through Europe. So he knows all of the Continent like a book! He went to Cornell University last year (NY) and then at the end of the school year, he bought a car and traveled through the United States visiting school friends and friends he had made on his tours. Spent the entire summer and has been <u>everywhere</u>!! He's returning to Oxford this fall to take his bar exams (lawyer). Loves America and wants to return to <u>live</u> there.

Colin (pronounced like Collin) Haycraft – fascinating little person! A real <u>individualist</u>! A writer – will work on a London newspaper this year. Also went to Oxford and spent this last year at Stanford Univ. Also very fond of America but will make his home in London. Short, dark, — magnificent accent and what a sense of humor!!! One of the quickest tongues I've ever heard – <u>so</u> <u>very</u> <u>clever</u>! We loved to be near him, because he kept us in constant laughter, and he's so intelligent!!

Bob Groow — older, about 38, used to be a Merchant Sea Captain. Tall, big, but very young acting! Also very English, but he has been living in Norfolk, VA for the last 3 years — still is something in the Navy. He is returning to visit his mother for 2 months.

Monica Pinnington – attractive girl engaged to Bob. Went to Norfolk to work. Is returning to visit her family, too. She's only 22, but suspect she and Bob will be married in England.

John Bennett and wife Betsy from Pittsburgh. Very charming.

—Rusty

Tony Short, Monica Pinnington, Bob Groow, Kit Tucker and I on board the Queen Mary. – Rusty

In addition to all the new people they met, Rusty and Kit enjoyed the daily routines of life on the *Queen Mary*. In her journal, Kit described how each morning the ship's paper, a puzzle, and the "Programme for To-day" were delivered. She also mentioned that a "little man comes around [and] bangs on pan to indicate first breakfast."

The *Queen Mary* was filled with amenities and no end of activities. Tourist class had its own pool, movie theatre, dance floor, and more. There was one amenity missing, however. Each room did not have a private bath. In order to wash, it was

NOTICES	R.M.S. "QUEEN MARY"	Sunday, September 12, 1954

PROGRAMME OF EVENTS

a.m.
8.00—" Name of Authors " Competition

10.00—Movie:	Cinema
" APACHE " Burt Lancaster and Jean Peters	

p.m.
2.00—Movie:	Cinema
" APACHE " Burt Lancaster and Jean Peters	

3.45—Music for Teatime	Winter Garden
Queen Mary String Orchestra, directed by Raoul Bacot	
3.45—Melody Time	Smoke Room
Charles Saxby at the Hammond Organ—relayed	
4.30—Movie:	Cinema
" APACHE " Burt Lancaster and Jean Peters	
6.00—7.00—Cocktail Music	Smoke Room
6.15—News Broadcast (British)	Winter Garden
6.30—News Broadcast (American)	Winter Garden
9.00—Orchestral Selections (relayed)	Winter Garden
Queen Mary String Orchestra, directed by Raoul Bacot	
9.15—KENO (Bingo-Lotto)	Smoke Room
9.30—Movie:	Cinema
" APACHE " Burt Lancaster and Jean Peters	
10.30—FAREWELL DANCE	Smoke Room
Queen Mary Dance Trio, directed by Barney Desmond	

CLOCKS
Clocks will be ADVANCED 20 minutes at 5.00 p.m., 11.00 p.m. and 2.00 a.m.

Passengers are kindly requested to remain in the accommodation allocated to the Class in which they are travelling

TOURIST CLASS

necessary to make an appointment with the Bath Stewardess (who drew the bath for you). There was a tub full of salt water in which to soak and a shower with fresh water in which to rinse off.

The "Programme for To-Day" listed the events offered that day: music, games, movies, and dancing among many other activities. The two girls embraced life on board the ship. They spent most of their time socializing, but they did manage to squeeze in a few movies. They watched: *The Green Scarf* (British, 1948), *The Red Shoes* (British, 1948), *Susan Slept Here* (American, 1954), *The Young Lovers* (British, 1954), and *Apache* (American, 1954).

Their progression of bedtimes was captured in Kit's journal: "We ended up at 4:00 am"; "Didn't get to bed until 5:00 am"; "Finally got to bed at 5:30"; "Finally got to bed at 6:30!"

Rusty described life on board as "<u>Wild</u> and <u>exciting</u> and <u>wonderful</u>!!!"

One aspect of traveling by ship is often foremost on people's minds – seasickness. Kit and Rusty were lucky in this respect. Their only brush with seasickness (on the *Queen Mary*, that is) came on their second full day on board. Rusty described their experience in a letter home:

> *Then – for the first time both Kit and I began feeling a little "queasy" — we hadn't taken any Dramamine that morning because we had felt so good the day before. We promptly took some and then Bob (who said you never "get used to it") took us in hand, and the 3 of us walked briskly back and forth on deck for half an hour in misty rain and wind. — Then it was lunch time, and he told us (as a billion others did) to <u>eat</u> lots! Very little liquids and foods that <u>stick</u> and "hold your stomach" down. So we did - felt <u>much</u> better and in an hour we felt wonderful, and never even felt a twinge after that!*
> *—Rusty*

While the girls enjoyed the amenities, events, and lack of seasickness, it is clear that the main attractions on the voyage were the young men from the U.K. Kit wrote:

> *We're getting a very nice crowd together – They're all English and all just wonderful characters – each one a great individualist – so unlike Amers who are all so much the same – These English boys have such marvelous senses of humor – Rusty and I could sit all day and be amused by them. Everything is very informal – we sit*

around in sports clothes with our feet up and talk and laugh and
dance – having a wonderful time. Chris gave me the rush tonight
and Rusty and I had a good chuckle over it since she was it last
night – we had already previously agreed after her experience with
him last night that he was a real operator but very charming and
amusing! —Kit

Staying up late agreed with Rusty and Kit. Only one disappointment occurred, due to keeping such late hours. On September 11, the girls went back to bed after breakfast, and, as a result, they missed seeing the RMS *Queen Elizabeth* sail past, as well as a few hours of sunshine. "Furious that we missed sun <u>and</u> Elizabeth," wrote Kit.

The consolation prize, however, was the SS *United States* sailing by later in the day. Kit and Rusty were quite excited to see her. Kit wrote, "Gave us a very funny feeling to watch her," and Rusty noted, "Everyone stood on deck and waved. ... Thrilling to see her and to see the Stars and Stripes sailing from her mast!"

That afternoon, they went with friends to the Mermaid Bar in Cabin Class and sipped a brandy. There they met three Americans who invited them back to their cabin for a party. Rusty described them as "all rah-rah college boys from Michigan State Univ ... they even had 3 stewards serving hors d'oeuvres, etc!" Later in the trip they ran into the boys in Copenhagen and swapped stories of their travels.

After the cocktail party with the Michigan boys, Rusty and Kit joined Chris Willy and Morris Tuck to go dancing. Morris had just finished one year of postgraduate work at the University of Indiana after graduating from the London School of Economics.

Rusty was with Morris and Kit with Chris. Rusty recounted (and illustrated) an amusing description of the dance floor:

> We danced a few dances in the Smoke Room and decided to try and "sneak in" to the Cabin Class dance. Several of us went. ... It rocked vigorously that night, but in a different way than ours did. It was easier to dance on this one but also funnier ... first you climb a hill, then you slide down. Everyone started singing and we really had a very gay and marvelous time. —Rusty

Kit Tucker and I in the sun! Aboard the Queen Mary. — Rusty

While Rusty wrote about the physical aspects of the dance floor, Kit wrote about the social aspects:

> Chris got huffy when I said I thought we ought to sit with Tony instead of dancing since we would have had to leave Tony all alone and Chris had said he was afraid Tony was mad at him because they had planned to go to the movies together and Chris had gone with me without telling Tony!! Sooo, bunch of us went over to Cabin

Class to their dance. Rusty was with Morris and I annexed his friend Colin Smallridge. Had a wonderful time dancing – they are both good dancers. Haven't danced so much in ages. The dance floor is very good and the band is excellent. Chris arrived with another girl and we ignored each other. —Kit

Kit and Rusty went to bed at 5:30 a.m. that night (morning), but they weren't in bed long. About 10 minutes later there was a knock at the door. Monica and her roommate wanted to know if they'd like to go watch the sunrise. Rusty wrote later:

At the stern the moon was low, golden yellow, and it was beautiful! The reflection in that vast body of water was like a vision! After a few dreamy moments we walked (2 blocks) to the bow and posted ourselves to watch the sunrise but clouds beat us to it. —Rusty

Kit added this in her journal:

It is so quiet then – the decks gleam with a quiet cold white and the prow of the ship cuts through the water so majestically well – it seems as though it is going on eternally and it seems impossible that there is anything beyond the horizon except more water and no other ship on the sea but yours. The engines rumble steadily and the water hisses past while the morning wind in the rigging screams or whines in gusts. We watched them change watch and finally when the sun didn't arrive we gave up and went back to Tourist Class – just dead! —Kit

After getting a few hours of sleep, they spent their last full day on the *Queen Mary* snapping pictures in First Class, having tea, and going to the movies. That night there was more dancing and Rusty "ended up with Colin H. that night. Had wonderful time – wish I could go into detail." After the dance, Chris, Kit, Colin and

Rusty walked on deck. Rusty offered this poetic description of the scene:

The full moon was gleaming silver; the entire sky was light with silvery puffs of clouds and a few twinkly stars. The ocean reflected this silvery light in every wave and ripple, giving the world an ethereal unreal quality – I felt we had somehow been transported into space and we no longer had any connection with earth. It was unbelievably beautiful and then we noticed a few lights to the North and a beacon from a lighthouse!! A sign of land! The first!!! Which was also a thrill! —Rusty*

The next day was their last on the ship. Rusty wrote, "Our gang clustered around us and followed us everywhere." The *Queen Mary* docked at Cherbourg, France, at 12:15 p.m. on Monday, September 13, 1954, before traveling on to Southampton, where Kit and Rusty's new English friends were headed. In Cherbourg, the two girls were the last ones off the ship.

Later in the trip, Chris Willy wrote the girls that the *Queen Mary* was a "morgue" after they got off in Cherbourg. Both girls wrote about Ronald, their table steward who had a bit of an Alec Guinness look to him, coming out of the dining room to say goodbye. They seemed quite touched by this and by overhearing one of the officials say, "My, what a lot of friends those girls made!"

Rusty captured the end of their voyage in a letter home to her mother, dated September 16, 1954:

As soon as we were off the ship hurrying to catch the train everyone was gibbering words I did not understand! We were in France!!!
—Rusty

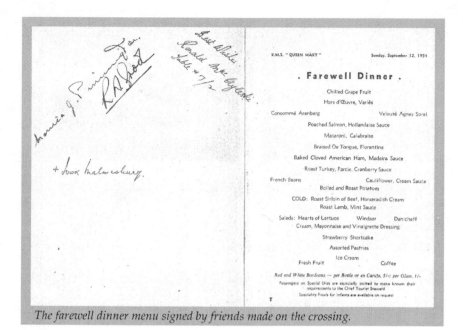

The farewell dinner menu signed by friends made on the crossing.

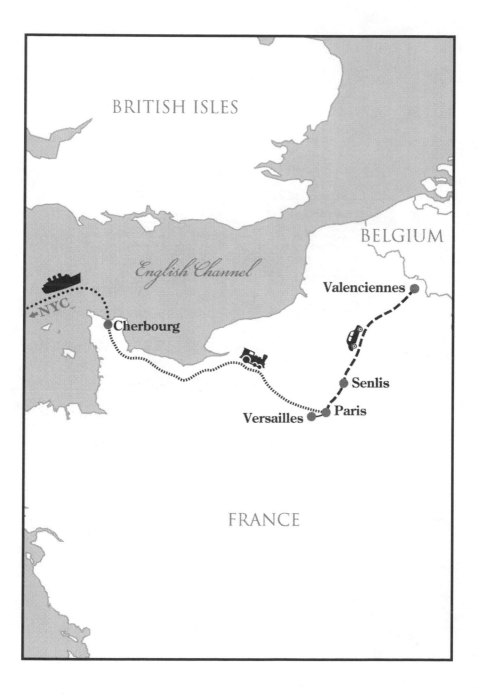

BRITISH ISLES

BELGIUM

English Channel

Valenciennes

NYC

Cherbourg

Senlis

Versailles Paris

FRANCE

FRANCE

*And in some beautiful farm, one building
would be lying in crumbled stone with perhaps
one wall standing, and we realized that here had
been War. Bombs. Men slipping through the
beautiful countryside to throw hand grenades at
a building harboring the enemy. Fear.
It sent chills through us.*

~Rusty Tyler

3

Taking the Train
Through Normandy
(September 13, 1954)

After all the planning and saving, the girls were finally on the Continent. In May 1954, Rusty had left New York and moved back home to save money for the trip. She worked with her mother at the Fort Pierre National Bank and read everything about Europe she could get her hands on. On September 2, she left South Dakota on a Greyhound bus and arrived in New York in time for her friend's wedding on September 4.

To raise money for the trip, Kit had continued working for NBC in New York. She asked for a three-month leave of absence starting in September.

The girls estimated the trip would cost them about $5 a day in addition to the cost of transportation. They bought tickets for the passage on the *Queen Mary* (about $165 each) several months in advance. Rusty (with her mother's help) paid around $1,295 (the MSRP) for a Renault 4CV, with plans to pick it up in Paris. She also bought car insurance. Kit agreed to pay for the gas. With American Express Travelers Cheques in their purses, the girls were ready for adventure.

They arrived on the Continent after crossing the narrow, windy gangplank from the ship onto land in Cherbourg, a port town located in the Normandy region of France. The girls ran to catch the train to Paris. "We made it to the train in a daze," wrote Kit. Hanging their heads out the window, the girls took one last look

A drawing included in a letter home by Rusty. It shows the type of well they passed in the French countryside

at the *Queen Mary* before catching glimpses of a damaged Cherbourg and a beautiful French countryside shattered by the effects of World War II.

Normandy is all country – green farms with cows, pigs, goats, etc. and lovely stone houses which have obviously been there for centuries. I think the first thing that impressed me was how green everything was, then how old the houses were. ... They all have flower gardens – even if there is only a little patch of dirt, and the house is about to fall into a pile of stones. —Kit

Rusty described the view outside the train window:

I couldn't believe my eyes! Quaint stone houses with red tile roofs, small French children in peasant dresses and aprons and dirty faces waving to us. Handsome young men on bicycles, waving. An old woman hauling up a bucket of water from an old stone well that resembled a wishing well. ... Old men, stooped, dressed in black, and all wearing berets ... all the land looked like thick green plush.
—Rusty

Charmed by the sights, the girls were sobered when confronted with evidence of war. Rusty continued her description of the sights outside the train's window:

And in some beautiful farm, one building would be lying in crumbled stone with perhaps one wall standing, and we realized that here had been War. Bombs. Men slipping through the beautiful countryside to throw hand grenades at a building harboring the enemy. Fear. It sent chills through us. —Rusty

When the train pulled into Gare St. Lazare in Paris, Kit, who spoke a little French, went to find a porter to help them with their suitcases. Rusty wrote about the station's mayhem, "What a Mad House! Swarms of people everywhere – everyone speaking a language I didn't understand – Cold, gray and cloudy and terribly exciting!!!"

[…]Everybody seemed to know where they were going and what they were saying except us – of course Rusty wasn't able to say anything and I was standing there looking around helplessly and mumbling "porteur" while nobody paid the slightest bit of attention to me. What a feeling – I was sure the train was going to pull out [with] all our stuff still on it, so finally Rusty handed the things out the window and I piled them up on the platform. —Kit

The girls were trying to figure out what to do when a familiar face appeared. Cherie, a friend of Kit's from New York, surprised them at the train. An American as well, Cherie had arrived in Paris three weeks before the girls. She was teaching children of American servicemen. Cherie's presence was comforting, but they still needed a porter. Kit wrote:

I annexed a porter (rather I guess I should say he annexed me). A real character – he sized me up right away as an inexperienced American dope whom it was his duty to assist. He piled our baggage into his truck (and if he could have, I think he would have tucked one of us under each arm) and we trundled off down the platform. It was quite a distance and we kept wandering off in the wrong direction – whereupon, he would click his tongue, shake his head furiously and shout, "No, no" at us. He found out that I spoke a little French and then we got along famously. —Kit

After Cherie helped them get a taxi, the girls were off, in Rusty's words, "zooming through the colorful, gaily lighted streets of Paris!"

There was no room to park in front of the hotel, so we pulled up a little ways and while Rusty and the driver unloaded, I ran into the hotel to get a porter. Of course, it is impossible to rush the French on anything like that and I probably scared the life out of them –

*running in – wild eyed – hair flying – a fistful of money in my hand
and mumbling incoherent French interspersed with English.* —Kit

For the next six nights, during what would be the first of two trips to Paris, the girls stayed at the Hotel France et Choiseul at 239 Rue Saint Honore in the 1st arrondissement in the most fashionable part of Paris. Rusty described it all in a letter to her mother:

It's very old, too; and so Continental! Lovely entrance! White marble and gold. Huge doors (like those on an old castle). And there is a darling open courtyard! White stone floor and little white iron tables and chairs – and a circular staircase, white marble with red carpeting.

Kit was very wonderful! What ever would I have done without her?? She managed with her French to at least make our wants understood to them! The men who helped us were a riot! Sooo French. From the train to our hotel room we encountered 5 men that helped us with our luggage and ourselves and to whom we had to give a tip!

[…] the Hotel sent out a tiny boy to carry in all our heavy suitcases. Then an old man took over. And 5 min. after we were in our rooms we heard this panting and huffing and puffing. Here was the old man carrying our suitcases one at a time. Of course most of the huffing was for our benefit and for a bigger tip. Very funny.
—Rusty

While the porter struggled with their luggage, the concierge led them to Room 6 on the second floor front, directly across the street from IBM and right next to the Georg Jensen store. Kit described their room:

Our room is large and comfy and OLD. It has faded pink and white wallpaper, twin brass beds, an immense wardrobe, dresser with marble top, sink, marble top fireplace, telephone and (big deal) <u>central heating</u>. (This means that there is a tiny radiator in one corner which will not be turned on until October. We both have colds already) and French window onto the street. For this we pay 15,000 francs a day or $4.35. This is considered a medium price hotel. —Kit

Kit in our first hotel room! Le France et Choiseul. Paris, France. — Rusty

Tired and hungry, the girls left the hotel in search of a bit of French nourishment. It was 9 p.m. and at least 12 hours since they had eaten anything.

Here we were — Miss Tucker and Miss Tyler walking on the streets of Paris, Sept. 13, 1954. ...We walked and walked completely dazed and unbelieving — in a big circle and back to our hotel without finding a café that we had the courage to enter. So started walking

down our street the Rue Saint Honore (Saint is pronounced Sah (nasal). Finally went into small place; open – which was a Tabac [a small bar that serves drinks, hard and soft, coffee, sandwiches, pastries, fruit, tobacco, stamps, etc.]. But quaint. So different from its equivalent in America. The man of course couldn't speak English. We had ham sandwiches on the most delicious bread I have ever tasted!!! Thick, thick hard crust! The inside is not soggy like French bread at home, and the flavor is magnificent!!! Butter is never served; and you don't want it! It would detract from the flavor of the bread. Everyday you meet people in the parks or walking down the streets who have a small loaf of bread; they just tear off pieces and eat it as they go. Wonderful! And we had café.
—Rusty

Kit wrote, "I had ordered mine with milk (café au lait) but Rusty ordered hers black – and WOW! It curls your hair, it's so strong!"

Still hungry, the girls continued down the street and found another café. They ordered *potage* (soup) which was brought in a gigantic tureen with a huge silver ladle.

We helped ourselves and each had 3 full soup dishes full. A loaf of bread was put on the table for each of us. (The loaves are about 2 inches by 1½ or 1-inch thick and most are about 3 feet long, but they make them small for restaurants. Ours were a little longer than this sheet of paper.) Then we had a café (coffee – French style) and a fresh peach "un pesche." Came home warm and comfortably very tired. Slept till 1:00 the next day – And felt very much revived!!!
—Rusty

4

Discovering Paris
(September 14, 1954)

"There is nothing like discovering something yourself because then it belongs entirely to you – the moment and the place are of your own creation – no one has planned it for you," Kit wrote in her journal at the end of their first full day in Paris. They would soon discover that their hotel was only 500 meters from Jardin Les Tuileries and Le Louvre.

After sleeping in until about 1 p.m. trying to overcome their lack of sleep, the girls unpacked. At 3 p.m., they left the hotel. They found "breakfast ... in a fascinating little 'patisserie' (French coffee shop where you can buy exquisite little cakes, cookies, buns, etc., — like nothing you've ever tasted in the USA)," wrote Rusty.

According to Kit, they each ate two eggs, bacon, French bread and coffee for 450 francs (about 60 cents) and then set out to discover Paris on a beautiful, sunny fall day. "We were on the

Kit in the Tulieres. — Rusty

town in Paris … didn't even know where we were so we bought a street map."

> *Looking down a little side street, we saw green trees and a fence at the end of it and decided to investigate. So – we wandered down the street and here was this immense park on a beautiful wide street with shops under an arcade on one side and the park on the other. We floated across the street – wide-eyed – and into the park and it turned out to be the most famous spot in Paris! The Tuileries! These are the gardens leading up to the Louvre Museum – most famous in the world.* —Kit

According to Rusty, the park was:

*Magnifique! Beautiful large park – formal gardens, Grecian marble
statues lining every path, flowers so brilliant we just gasped! Never
have I seen such colors!!! We still haven't been able to figure what
has made them so. It must be the air, or a special light that the sun
casts over Paris alone.* —Rusty

Both Kit and Rusty were struck by the brilliant colors of the
flowers in the Tuileries and in all of Paris.

*The flowers glow with a brilliant intensity which seems to burst
from within. The reds are bursting flame and the yellows look as
though they were plucked from the heart of the sun. ... In the
Tuileries they have grouped all these brilliant colors together along
the edges of the beds – they have reds, yellow, blue and greens
massed together and each color seems to play upon the other until –
as you look at them, they seem to build into a glorious burst of
harmony in color and song.* —Kit

Finding a couple of small, wire-backed chairs in the park, Rusty
and Kit sat down to study the map and the people. According to
Rusty, "The park was full of French people – one couple sat on a
bench near us and the little old man in beret and 'goatee' kept
turning around to 'stare' subtly at us."

*Little French children were everywhere playing happy French
games – rolling hoops with long sticks, and sailing boats in a pretty
pond. An old woman stood nearby with a sort of a wheelbarrow
loaded with large sailboats that she was renting or selling to the
children. All the little boys in France wear short cuffed pants – their
legs are so brown, and they look so cute. They must be 12 or 13 or
more before they wear long pants, and I like it! Wish American boys*

did that. And all the little girls in a family are dressed like twins –
just alike - same with the boys in a family. —Rusty

While Rusty described the children, Kit wrote about the adults
at the park:

The mothers or nurses sit around and knit and talk madly in French
(naturally). At lunch time they pull out a long loaf of French bread,
some fruit, cheese and "what have you" – and eat right there. It is
really delightful – they are such a practical people. If they get
hungry – they eat right where they are! —Kit

Rusty and Kit stood out as the American tourists they were.
Rusty wrote, "We passed two French boys (about 14 years old)
and they laughed and Kit heard them say – "Ahhh – les
Americains!" How can they tell?!!!!"

The girls were meandering about Paris, with little purpose and
scarcely an agenda, when the Eiffel Tower came into view.

I looked up at the sky because it seemed to be getting cloudy and
there – standing against a piling mass of gray and white clouds, was
the Eiffel Tower! I told Rusty to look at the sky – she gasped and we
both stood there in the middle of the busy sidewalk and grinned like
idiots while the French people walked by – looked at us tolerantly –
nudged each other and said "Les Américaines!" —Kit

The girls walked along the wide street of the Champs Élysées,
admiring the trees and gardens along the way. They stopped for
lunch before walking up to the Arc de Triomphe. Rusty was
overwhelmed. "As we suddenly saw the flowers on the Tomb of

the Unknown Soldier, and the eternal light burning, chills went all over both of us, a funny feeling inside, and tears came to my eyes."

Kit penned in her journal, "It is difficult to describe the feeling of actually seeing a thing you have heard about all your life but it really does something to you to see the Tomb of the Unknown Soldier."

The Eiffel Tower and I. (ha) Paris September 15, 1954. - Rusty

The whole day was simply enchanting, according to Kit, as the girls walked across Paris, stopping to look in shop windows, to shop in Au Printemps, a big department store, and to admire the city.

Had a few things to buy so went to a new department store (new to us, that is) – And what a store!! Really huge, and the inside was round; and when standing in the middle and looking up, it was like *looking up from the center of the main floor of the capitol building at home – only much enlarged. Each floor (eleven in all!) was like an open balcony … and the dome at the top was glass to let the daylight in – wild really! – Very <u>modern</u>, gently spiraled staircases curled up to the first floor; — And <u>then</u>!! Ascending, like little bugs, were the elevators – they were covered in red velvet and looked as though they were <u>crawling</u> up the side of the balconies from one floor to another! We took one to the 11th floor and down and I felt like I was at Coney Island – It was scary, because there was "glass all" round at eye level, and you were hanging out over the side … where you looked way down below and the elevator started to move – <u>quite</u> a <u>thrill</u>!* —Rusty

"Paris must be the most fascinating and beautiful city in the world," Kit wrote. "It even <u>smells</u> different."

The next day, the girls set out toward the Place de la Concorde, just an 650-meter walk from their hotel. Rusty described the Place de la Concorde in a letter to her mother entitled, "Paris Edition, Chapter 3."

It's huge! In the center is the famed Cleopatra's needle; nearby is a lovely large marble fountain; Standing beside the "needle," you look first to the north and there are lovely large marble buildings far ahead … some of the Embassies are there, including the American Embassy. And what [a] thrill it is to see the Stars and Stripes flying out in front! Cars are zooming every which way all around the large circle in which we are standing; and to our right and to our left, across the area where the cars are scurrying, are tall lovely statues, each one representing a major city in France. … Paris is the most beautiful, of course. … To the right are the Tuileries, the lovely, beautiful gardens and far, far down is the small Arch of Triumph, and behind that is the great Louvre, spreading out its arms magnificently and powerfully. Looking south, there is a tall gate, a long path, and des Invalides, looking like a lovely Napoleonic palace that we shall investigate soon. Turning toward the West, finally, is the indescribable Champs Élysées, rightly vain for it knows it holds the title of the most beautiful Avenue in the World. Two white marble statues stand at either side of the entrance and you are drawn toward the lovely boulevard, gasping as you look up to see the Arc de Triomphe, far down at the end. There simply are no words. —Rusty

As Kit took a picture of the Arc de Triomphe from the Place de la Concorde, she was struck by the layers of history merging on a daily basis in the lives of Parisians. She wrote in her journal:

It really is fantastic to stand there in the center and watch all the funny little French cars whizzing madly round and round and think that several hundred years ago Marie Antoinette was being beheaded on the very spot! ... This was really the feeling theme for the day because next we crossed the Seine to L'Hotel des Invalides and Napoleon's tomb. —Kit

A former veteran's hospital, Hotel des Invalides houses Napolean's tomb and is known as Europe's greatest military museum. The museum is located at 129 Rue de Grenelle and includes displays on both world wars. Rusty described the museum:

But then we turned away for we wanted to see Des Invalides, a ... kind of foreboding stone "palace." We entered an archway and stood in a large bare gray square. Great stone pillars stood sentinel on all four sides; ancient and modern cannon lay tumbled near the walls, and some lay forgotten on the open cobblestone square. Each footstep echoed in this great stone square which Napoleon built for his triumphant armies. And suddenly you hear, ghostlike, the echoing victorious cries, the cheers, and the gay loud voices of strong gaily decorated men. Colorful uniforms, flashing blades of steel. Napoleon and his men in all their glory.

The visions and the echoes fade, a century passes and the square is frightening and cold and you hear Hitler's armies marching into Paris taking over this square and dominating it with heels clicking goosesteps on the cobblestones, and rough Nazi orders being bitten off the tongues of men as cruel and unfeeling as the gray stone walls about them.

Ghosts continued to dance about us, as we hurried down to an archway and escaped with a shudder. Before us was a lovely formal garden. And the entrance to Napoleon's tomb. What a breath taking sight as we climbed the marble stairs inside. The main "room" is all in white marble, large and round with the center, of course, sunk way down. Behind this sunken circle is an altar, bathed in a rich golden light - it seems far away and mystical. The high dome is ornate but lovely – and you suddenly feel that you have come into the presence of Greatness. In awe you are drawn to the center. There it is. But it is almost ugly. Which perhaps is fitting for there on a marble pedestal is a "casket" of dark red marble – very smooth and very shiny. The shape is very scrolly and – I was disappointed though as I said, it seemed rather almost fitting – for, though he was a genius in his own right, he was also rather hideous. In the midst of the great things he did for Paris, he did evil and cruel things to other nations and other peoples.

We stand and gazed for a long time then walked around near the altar — What a start we got there!! Behind the figure of Christ on the cross was a large misty window and through it we could see ethereally, the bare threads and decay of many flags hanging. ... It sent a slight shiver of horror through us ... strangest thing. To know they have been hanging there long enough for the material simply to disintegrate and leave only a net of threads. Brrr — Later we found that flags are hanging that way all over Europe!! Behind the altar were steps going down to where the marble encased Napoleon lay. Encircling the bier were statues of Napoleon in the various roles he played: as wise man, as Emperor, as benefactor, as scholar, as judge, etc. And the story of what he did for France was written on white marble plaques. Kit read them all and translated for me. Such a tiny little man – what a genius he really was – but then to have so much power! And after all that – there he lay, encased in red marble in a gigantic sepulcher – that seemed like a vain attempt to hold on to his power or his influence; but he is only ashes; nothing can alter that, and he is actually on a level now with every other being that has lived and died. Seeing all this and Napoleon made me very thoughtful. ... We remained there a long time. —Rusty

5

Exploring the Left Bank and the Latin Quarter
(September 15 – September 16, 1954)

The girls left Hotel des Invalides hungry. It was 2 p.m. as they wandered across the city into a "marvelous" old section of town on the Left Bank which Rusty described as having "Narrow, winding streets not slums but definitely a poorer section! Little alleyways led back to tiny courtyards choked with hanging laundry, boxes, garbage, and cats."

Called "La Rive Gauche" in French, the six arrondisements of the Left Bank are located on the southern side of the Seine. The Left Bank includes the Latin Quarter (located in the 5th and 6th arrondisements).

After choosing a *tabac*, Rusty and Kit went into the back room and sat at a table. Kit described it as dirty and really grubby. Rusty wrote:

And then a man came to ask us what we wanted who looked exactly like a dissipated James Mason. I don't think he had ever seen an American before! We ordered just bread and cheese, and we watched as he picked up a two-yard loaf of bread that had been standing, leaning against a door frame! Whacked with a cleaver, two enormous chunks. While we ate the crunchy bread and delicious cheese and drank hot strong French coffee, we were intrigued by this James Mason character who kept talking to a cat which lay under one of the tables. And a girl ("waitress") appeared terribly French and she looked as if she was kept locked up in a garret when she wasn't working. It was a perfect setting for a movie! A good Hitchcock movie. ... We were completely fascinated by it! —Rusty

In spite of the rain, Kit and Rusty moved on toward Champs de Mars and the Eiffel Tower. Kit wrote that she had never been so wet. Her red shoes were soaked, and the dye stained her feet pink. Kit wrote that night in her journal:

We are getting to be old hands at the Metro. Even changed trains tonight! They have signs in the car reminding passengers that it is criminal to let old people or pregnant women or children under 4 stand! Also, as soon as a train enters the station they close the gate so nobody has to run! It really is delightful. Oh, there are so many things we keep noticing every day and meaning to take notes of but there are too many! The children are wonderful – they play with such simple toys – a hoop, ball, stick. And are really amused and happy. —Kit

Kit and Rusty joined Kit's friend Cherie for dinner in the Latin Quarter the balmy night of September 15. Rusty wrote about their "high heels clicking on the pavement" and their "little gasps of excitement" as they neared the "dark and lustrous" Seine River. She wrote, "We stood by its side and gazed down the lighted twisting way of the poetic Seine."

The infamous "arty" section – walked past the Sorbonne University ... students were milling about – even at that hour. Then we got lost – or at least Cherie couldn't remember just which direction we wanted to go – So we finally gave up and climbed into a very "French" Parisienne taxi. Two seconds and we were there – at "La Pergola" a fascinating little restaurant in the midst of the student section. And supposed to be the place where "existentialism" was born. —Rusty

"Very good – very atmosphere – very dirty!" Kit wrote about La Pergola on Rue St. Germain in her journal. "Saw at least 4 cockroaches on the railing next to me! I've got to get over my horror if I am to enjoy myself! Meal was quite expensive." While Kit was getting over her horror at seeing insects, Rusty was entranced with the atmosphere and the people.

There were a few tables outside on the sidewalk; and the downstairs room (small) contained a bar, tables, a jukebox playing French songs and French adaptations of American songs, and people! Girls with long straight ponytails, turtle necked black sweaters; men with thick long hair, also wearing turtle necked sweaters, and slim legged trousers all looking very artistic or studious or ? Terribly intriguing anyway. We climbed some stairs and sat at a rickety wooden table overlooking the downstairs room. I leaned over the balcony during most of the meal – watching the gay activity — The dinner was quite good, particularly the onion soup; magnificent flavor – many onions, thick crusty top and wonderful cheese – the best I have ever tasted anywhere!!! Then we had delicious French steak, fresh green beans, a salad, "French" fried potatoes! And a peach for dessert. Hated to leave. But Cherie said she had another place she wanted us to go – so we squeezed our way past "flirting" young French men and walked down more small alley like streets. ... —Rusty

Between two tall buildings, the girls and Cherie stumbled upon a play being performed in a vacant lot.

There was a small picket fence and two policemen standing nearby. A large crowd was seated on folding chairs and an improvised stage with costumed players could be seen at the far end. Appropriately they were doing Molière! (a French playwright of the Elizabethan Age – we spent a whole quarter at Northwestern studying him). —Rusty

"Then Cherie took us to a place called l'Abbaye. Fabulous!" Kit wrote.

Tiny, smoky ... drank 2 glasses of wine until 1:30 am. Cherie took a cab and Rusty and I started to walk – in wrong direction of course – finally got going right but picked up 5 French lads who followed us all the way home – took us about ¾ of an hour to walk back! Finally made it but oh what a trial! Wonderful, wonderful evening though. Wonderful, wonderful life – can't believe it! —Kit

6

Picking Up a Car in Paris
(September 17 – September 18, 1954)

When Rusty began planning a trip to Europe, she saw an advertisement in the newspaper to buy a car in the U.S., a 1955 Renault 4CV, and pick it up in Europe. With financial help from her mother, Rusty ordered the car from home. Now it was time to claim it. With international drivers' licenses obtained from the Touring Club of France, the girls were ready to pick up the car. "We are to pick up the car Friday afternoon and expect to take off Saturday. Ulp!" Kit wrote.

On Friday, they took the Metro to the Renault office where they met Paul, a man whom Kit described as "just the right size for a Renault." Kit wrote, "We had a hilarious ride over with his Eng and my French. He was really darling – took us through Bois de Boulogne – just beautiful! And bought us coffee at a gorgeous café."

Another 20 minutes and we were at the Renault factory ... !!! I was really so excited. I wanted to <u>turn</u> <u>and</u> <u>run</u>! I was scared. The strangest feeling — I had never owned a car before. ... In the office I was given all kinds of papers and instruction books, etc. – And Paul (I can't remember the little Frenchman's last name) and I looked among the <u>rows</u> of Renaults for a light green one with a sunshine roof that would have my name on it — And hidden back in a corner – there she was!! Men in coveralls pushed her out, shined her up, filled her with gas, whizzed her out on the street – and there she was — All mine! Was "scared to death" of her – She was so <u>tiny</u>!! — Then Paul tried to explain everything to me and show the various "things" and where they were located. ... But of course, — he didn't know the English words for all the "instruments," and Kit didn't know the French – so it got terribly funny — Finally he just would take my hand and put it on whatever he wanted to explain. ... <u>And</u> <u>then</u> he climbed in, told Kit to get in the back seat and off we went – <u>Me</u> <u>driving</u>! You have no idea how hard it was to drive!! I couldn't judge any distance at all. ... And I began to decide I'd never get used to it. (But – I did soon enough – And how! – Whoosh! Wheeeee!)

After going around the block a few times, we zoomed off along, following Monsieur Paul in his car – through whizzing Parisienne traffic — And to his office again. It was 6:00 PM by this time and the height of rush hour. —Rusty

Kit wrote in her journal, "Rusty was terrific on the way back – driving in huge traffic. It was so bad when we got to the garage that we decided to leave it there and pick it up tomorrow. ... After much handshaking and Merci etc., etc. we wandered off in a happy daze."

Kit's international driver's license.

After their car buying adventure, the girls were hungry and stopped to buy a few groceries before finding a café for dinner.

> *Bought tomatoes at a marvelous vegetable stand where they wrap everything in newspaper. Little man saw me with my French phrase book and asked to see it – he proceeded to try and read some English – he pronounced "noisy" exactly as it would be pronounced in French. It was wonderful! Everybody got such a big kick out of it. Then bought some wonderful little cookies at a Patisserie – wandered some more and bought map of France, corkscrew, two plastic glasses, a knife, French – Eng dictionary. And finally – most exciting – a French string bag! We dumped all our newspaper wrapped parcels in it and decided all we needed was a loaf of French bread sticking out the top!* —Kit

Excitedly we went whistling down the street. … Were starving, so stopped in a cute little café and were ordering when two Frenchmen walked in, sat at the table right next to ours, and eventually they began to talk to us – about politics of all things – and why did Dulles go to every other European capitol except Paris – etc. – Kind of interesting – but then, inevitably, they wanted to buy our dinner for us. We said no in sixty different ways – trying to explain that we could still continue with our conversation, etc. And that in America it was "different." Etc. – But finally they left – without having their dinner, because we wouldn't let them pay for our dinner! I would have been only too happy to have let them pay for it if there wouldn't be the inevitable complications afterwards – The usual attached-to-a–string business. … They were quite charming – the truly gallant Frenchmen – you would have liked them! The definitely Charles Boyer type!! (ha!) —Rusty*

Had veal chop, gorgeous huge helping of string beans, wine in a cold stoneware pitcher and 8 different petits fours. The best I have ever eaten! Whole thing was about $1.65! —Kit*

We walked the loooong way home, stopping for glace at a little corner stand-place heavily gilded and decorated with lush art. … The glace is the ice cream of France, only it isn't ice cream – it's more like our ice – not sherbet, but ice – Only better. I had maple — and Kit had lemon (or "citron" which was cooling, not sweet, and really delicious!) – Had fun with the men behind the "bar" – And a big thrill: when a little American man and his wife asked us in labored French, where a particular Metro was. You should have seen their faces when we answered in English! —Rusty*

Saturday, the girls woke to rain, and set off to pick up the car they soon nicknamed "Europa." Rusty wrote about the rain on a postcard to her mother, "And the rain in Paris is so soft and fine – No one seems to mind or pay any attention to it – It adds to the complete charm of the city."

> *And Europa was duly christened with Parisienne rain! Somehow we made it back to our hotel, parked Europa, sparkling new and shining in the rain, in the large Place Vendome. Still seemed like a dream and we kept wanting to run back there all the rest of the day and make sure she was really there.* —Rusty

That night, their last evening in Paris, the girls bought "luscious" patisserie and a couple of rosy apples and wandered down to the Tuileries around 6 p.m.

> *Sat on a little white iron bench at the foot of a graceful white marble statue, and ate our supper at dusk as the lights began to come on – walked around the gardens, and beneath the small Arch of Triumph, turning to look far down through the misty light at the large Arc. … And in silent awe we approached the enormous Louvre, standing in almost frightening majesty – The size of the Louvre is almost beyond comprehension. … The soft darkness of Paris, a new falling mist and the gas-lamps casting a hazy glow about, make it very easy for our minds to run rampant again and go spinning back through Time. … Slowly we walked past the Louvre to the Seine, — out onto a bridge and stood looking down at the inky water and along its banks twinkling with many lights, felt the fine wet mist on our faces, soft and filmy - and vowed eternal love to Paris.* —Rusty

Kit and Rusty worried their luggage wouldn't fit in the little Renault. After much French and English discussion, the porters somehow managed to squeeze it all in the car. "The car, you know, is the smallest one made," Kit wrote.

> *We have in the back seat: my suitcase (on the floor), my carpak,*
> *Rusty's Pullman case, my hatbox, Rusty's train case, Rusty's*
> *plastic bag full of coats, 2 string bags with all our maps, etc., and a*
> *plastic bag with our eating equipment and food and my gray coat.*
> *Everything is scientifically arranged so that we can see out the back*
> *mirror. Oh – the luggage compartment is in the front (motor in the*
> *back) and is just large enough for Rusty's medium sized suitcase*
> *and our spare tire. —Kit*

Kit in the passenger seat of Europa.

After five nights in Paris, the girls settled their bill at Hotel France et Choiseul and began their road trip. Tickled that Europa's license plate number (1576TTA7S) included their initials, the girls promptly named their journey, "The Tucker Tyler Adventure." With Rusty driving and Kit navigating, they left Paris and set off for Versailles, the first of many stops along the way to Rome, their final destination.

7

Viewing Versailles
(September 19 - September 20, 1954)

With directions from the men at the Renault Factory, on September 19, 1954, Rusty and Kit began their driving tour of Europe. It began in grand fashion as they left Paris and headed straight to Versailles in their little Renault. Rusty wrote home:

> *There are many more Renaults in Paris than there are Fords in New York or anywhere!!! But they are tiny! You don't realize how tiny they are until you see it next to another car! Will send you a picture of it as soon as I can! It's a little darker green than this paper and a very pretty shade!!! And it is the <u>1955</u> model; which won't even be shown until the end of October. It has so many gadgets!* —Rusty

Both the girls were ecstatic about the car. Rusty described driving on their way out of Paris with exclamations such as "Wheeeeeeee" and "It's just like a TOY!" Kit was the navigator for this part of the journey with her lap "piled high with French maps."

> *Paris is really maddening! Ever hear stories about Paris drivers? Well – if you did – they are all TRUE! There are practically no traffic lights and in nine cases out of ten it is a case of who gets there first. Really - I have NEVER, never seen anything like it.*
> —Kit

The lunch they ate that day was somewhat less ostentatious than the palace they were about to visit, as Kit described in her journal:

> *Oh, almost forgot – had the first of what is to be the order of the day for lunch: ate French bread, cheese, tomato and patisserie for lunch in the car. Tasted wonderful – we got the giggles wondering what our families would think if they could see us.* —Kit

Both girls were in awe of the size and beauty of Versailles focusing in particular on the gardens and the fountains. Rusty described the overall experience of being there in a letter home:

> *It is all so beautiful! Soooo huge!!! And to think someone <u>lived</u> there! And the <u>cobblestones</u> that were there when Louis XIV lived in luxury and when they came there to get Marie Antoinette and Louis and behead them – Thinking of the history of it all – and the people who stood where we were standing and touched the things we were touching, sent chills and tingles up our spines.* —Rusty

After spending six and a half hours at Versailles, they still felt there was more to see and resolved to return when they came back to Paris later in the trip.

Kit and me at Versailles (rainy). — Rusty

Rusty and Kit continued north and headed for a small town just outside of Paris named Senlis to spend the night. They picked the Hotel du Nord from the Michelin guide, but they arrived late at night and almost did not get a room. Kit wrote in her journal, "Just as we got there they turned out all the lights so I leaped out and banged on the door. It opened and I mumbled some garbled French. I was let in and a flashlight showed me the way to the desk." Notably this part was left out of the letters home. To her parents, Kit just said, "We are now reposing in an adorable old place. We have bedroom and bath (immense tub!) hot, hot water and double bed – marvelously comfortable … and it is SPOTLESS!"

Well – we awoke the next morning and upon looking out of our French windows, we saw the most charming, most ancient little town imaginable! … Everything is made of stone – all the streets

*are cobblestone and very narrow and winding. It is as neat as a pin.
… There is nothing extra sitting around – NEVER any papers
flying around or garbage sitting around the streets. It is really
incredible! The houses come right down to the edge of the narrow
little streets and a great many of them have a wall in front of them.
Sometimes, as you go by, the little door in the wall is open and
inside you can see tiny, beautiful gardens – a riot of color and dogs
and cats. It is such a contrast to the rather bare, frugal looking
exterior. … We walked around all morning whispering – once in a
while we would see somebody, but mostly it was as though it was a
deserted city. Then – at 12:00 noon – doors opened and people
appeared on street corners all over. Children dashed madly about
and people appeared on bicycles. As we walked around, we were the
object of great interest and speculation. The children were most
interested in trying out their school English on us (they all take it)
and one darling little boy in shorts and sandals came up to us and
in a piping little voice said, "English is spoken?" We laughed and
said, "Yes."He said "Hello" – giggled and ran away.* —Kit*

In a letter home about this part of the trip, Kit observed of
France - "how much more emphasis there is upon the first world
war, than upon the second." She wondered at the ubiquitous
plaques commemorating people and events from World War I
versus the "small pathetique reminders of the second war" even
though it had been nearly 10 years since World War II ended.

By early afternoon, Kit and Rusty were on their way again. This
time they headed to Valenciennes to stay at the Buffet Hotel for
the night on their way to Brussels. They drove through towns in
which they noted the old buildings were made of stone, and the
new ones were made of red brick. Again, their road lunch

consisted of French bread ("a yard long"), cheese, fruit and French pastries eaten under an apple tree along the highway. After lunch, though, the real excitement began as Kit took on a long driving stretch. She described her first foray behind the wheel in her journal:

> *After lunch I drove for 3 hours! Imagine I must have given Rusty a couple of scares cause I came damn close to a couple of difficulties but she was very patient and calm about it – I'm sure I wouldn't have been. Anywho – I loved driving – hope I'll be okay.* —Kit

Kit Tucker walking up a street in Senlis, near the cathedral.
– Rusty

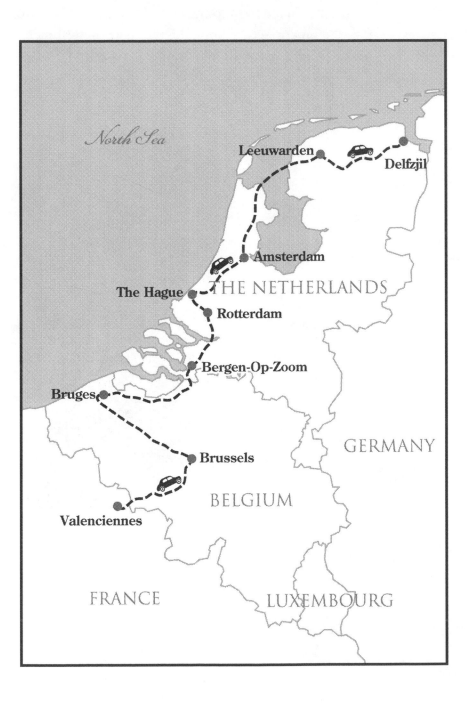

Belgium and The Netherlands

Did I tell you that after we have finished our trip with all this wonderful food, that we will be walking ads for the old slogan that "Travel is Broadening?"

~Kit Tucker

8

Smuggling in and out of Belgium
(September 21 – September 23, 1954)

Knowing they would return later to Paris, Rusty and Kit left the Buffet Hotel in Valenciennes, France, on the morning of September 21 and headed north along the coast through Belgium and The Netherlands on their way to Scandinavia.

We were driving gaily along a cobblestone street through a small town when we saw a gate to be lowered ahead – Rusty slowed down thinking it was a train gate – were we ever surprised when a man in uniform walked up and asked for our passports – French customs! We had no idea it was so close. Man asked Rusty for her "carnet" of ownership for the car so she pulled out all her papers and began going through them, holding up each one and he would say "non." Finally found what he wanted in the big envelope under the seat. They were very nice – didn't ask any questions about declaring money, valuables, etc. Belgian customs next. Same procedure – all the officials very sweet as we smiled brilliantly at them. As we drove merrily away, I suddenly looked down and there was the bottle of brandy we had bought sticking out from under the seat – gales of laughter. Our first trip through customs and we had unwittingly smuggled something through! —Kit

However, they were not yet done talking to men in uniform that day. As the girls entered Brussels they experienced their first traffic stop. Kit explained in her journal:

… Stopped by a policeman as we were entering the city – Rusty went thru a signal or something. Pulled over and a young handsome Belgian officer came over – I tried to explain the street we wanted. When he finally understood he said "American Express?" We said "Yes!" He said (in perfect English) "Why didn't you say so!" He then directed us. We went over and inquired about a place to stay. They were wonderful. The woman recommended a place and called up immediately for a reservation for us… and it is magnificent. Very imposing entrance. If we had wandered in off the streets we would have gone right out again because it is so elegant looking – we have an excellent room – twin beds (the mattresses tilt up at the head and have big pillows too!), blue wallpaper which looks like damask and damask blue drapes held by gold silken cords – two large sinks, dressing table, writing table and blue velveteen chair! Fabulous for $4.00 a night ($2.00 ea.) Went sightseeing in afternoon. —Kit

The hotel in Brussels was apparently the highlight of the city given Kit's enthusiastic description of the room followed by an analysis of the carpeting on the stairs.

The blue and gold Brussels carpeting is held in place at the back of each stair tread by heavy, flat, brass rods which look like swords – a

really striking effect. Actually all the hotels hold their carpeting down in this manner but usually the rods are more utilitarian looking. These are very handsome and someone must have to polish them every other day to keep them so brilliant. —Kit

The girls only spent one night in Brussels. In the morning it rained non-stop so they sat in the hotel lobby and wrote letters. When it was time to leave the city, it was still raining.

We left Brussels in rain and traffic at 5:30 – horrible!! Couldn't find our way out of the city to the right highway and we went round in circles!!! Traffic was hideous, streets were so tiny and so chopped up. – Was I relieved to get out of there!!! —Rusty

On their way out of Brussels, Kit and Rusty stopped by a market and bought "supper supplies" which Kit detailed in a letter home:

[…] Bought a big bunch of carrots, big bunch of immense, deep purple grapes, several luscious, red, ripe tomatoes and a loaf of dark brown bread. All these things cost about 35 cents in American money. You have never seen fruit and vegetables and flowers like they have over here. Everything is just lush – that's the only word for it – delicious tasting – not like California stuff. Oh! Did I ever tell you about the artichokes? Well – they are everywhere! And are the biggest, roundest, most wonderful looking things you have ever seen. I almost go mad because I can't buy them and take them home and cook them! —Kit

At the recommendation of the concierge at their hotel in Brussels the night before, Rusty and Kit headed for Bruges. They arrived in the city around 8:00 p.m., parked the car at the end of a canal, and set off straight away for the recommended hotel. Near the hotel they heard Mendelssohn's "Wedding March" being played by a carillon. Later Kit wrote home that they "had a nice room and bath WITH A JOHN! – our first private one in Europe! The bath is very modern – all black and white tile. We got the giggles when we saw it – such a change from all the others."

Kit in Bruges beside one of the many picturesque canals. – Rusty

The girls got up early the next morning in order to do some sightseeing. Both were taken in by the town – describing the bridges and canals, the adorable little houses, trees and flowers and horses. Rusty was tickled at the sight of the many painters along the canals. She wrote home:

There were painters standing all along the canals, wearing berets,
big floppy bow ties, — One was magnificent! He had a small gray
beard and moustache, tam, floppy suit, and was standing with
brush and palette in hand – his easel with half finished picture of
canal and tiny bridge — and a bicycle beside him. —Rusty

In a letter to her parents, Kit described the first stop on their
little tour of the city – the ascent of Belfort, the 366-step belfry
tower of Bruges.

Had no idea what we were getting into. It took us ten minutes of
steady climbing – going round and round and round and up a
narrow stone staircase which winds through the center column of
the tower (Kate Smith would NEVER make it!) Half the lights were
out and we had to feel our way. —Kit

At the top of the Belfort, Kit and Rusty decided the climb was
well worth it.

What a view from the top though! ... The city is like a fairy tale
come alive! It is made up of clusters of lovely, odd-shaped little
houses with red tile roofs, old churches and local museums. There
are many winding, dreamy canals with trees and bright flowers and
backyards hanging over them – and – on the little lakes at the ends
of them – swim graceful, snow white swans. There are, of course,
dozens of tiny humped stone bridges over the canals, and it seems as
though every time you turn a corner, there is another beautiful
grouping of houses, church, trees, flowers, etc. We took many
pictures, since for a change, the sun was shining. —Kit

After sightseeing in Bruges, Rusty and Kit settled back into
Europa and headed to The Netherlands. Crossing a border meant
going through customs again. The girls had read somewhere that

only one bottle of alcohol was allowed duty free. In the car was a bottle of wine and a bottle of brandy. Their solution? Start drinking, of course! As Rusty drove, Kit set about trying to open the wine bottle but had difficulty. Kit described the scene to her parents in a letter:

We had just decided finally to pull over so I could get out and try it standing up – when we pulled up to another <u>railroad</u> gate. I still had the bottle clutched between my knees when – suddenly – we realized it wasn't a railroad – IT WAS OF COURSE, "CUSTOMS"! Much earlier than we had expected and there was the little man approaching us! We both turned green, I am sure, and I frantically shoved the bottle under my seat and draped my brown pleated skirt gracefully around it. We smiled brilliantly at the man and handed over passports and car papers. He smiled and a couple of his buddies came over too. We had a lovely conversation about America and Belgium with lots of laughter in between because we couldn't understand them and they couldn't understand us! The rule is: if you don't understand what the other person is saying – you smile – if he smiles a little back – then you are both having a wonderful time. If he doesn't smile back you say "Ummm" or click your tongue. This shows you are sympathetic and then you understand each other… went through the same procedure at Dutch customs … we decided that if they asked us to get out so they could look – we would simply laugh and ask one of them if they wouldn't get the cork out of the bottle for us – since we were not strong enough. We didn't have to though. —Kit

9

Hearing Rubinstein in Holland
(September 23 – September 27, 1954)

Funny incident today – We were unprepared for Customs again. – They seem to suddenly pop up out of nowhere. – So after smiling our way out of Belgium and into Holland, — we had driven 50 feet and suddenly Kit grabbed my arm and said, "My God, we're in Holland!!" And that's just about the way we felt! And at that we both burst out into hysterical laughter. —Rusty

Rusty and Kit continued north into The Netherlands and spent the night in a town called Bergen-op-Zoom (a name which continually inspired giggles). Rusty described the sights along the way in a letter home to her mother on September 24:

The trip between Bruges, Belgium, and Bergen-op-Zoom, Holland, was delightful – and I kept thinking of you and how much you would love this!! Passed many windmills!!! And the people!! ¾ of the men are in wooden shoes! I can't get over it!! I thought they just wore those when they dressed up in costume on holidays or

*something, — but they don't. They wear them to work. And you
should see the men in their full pants and wooden shoes, pedaling
furiously on their bicycles! And the women! We saw more varieties
of the white caps – some <u>huge</u> white starched things that looked like
wings, — some tall white peaks, — and some were small – some
even had shiny "reflectors" attached to each side. We couldn't
decide if that was really part of the cap, or whether they were for
riding bicycles at night! – (ha!) And <u>several</u> were wearing the floor*

Drawing by Rusty of Dutch fashion in a letter home to her mother.

*(or top-of-the-shoe) length skirts, with white lace shawls, I guess
they are. It's a triangular lace shawl that they just x in front and
tuck the ends in. They are all very very plump!! And with these
clothes on, it's like looking in a <u>picture</u> <u>book</u>!! And they ride
bicycles, too. Driving along, we would suddenly see ahead of us this
huge round thing on a bicycle with a huge white hat that seemed to*

have wings that flapped in the breeze – And it would be only a woman on a bicycle. (My hand aches again.) —Rusty

At 7:30 p.m., after taking a ferry from Breskens to Vlissingen and driving along the islands off the Dutch coast, Rusty and Kit arrived in Bergen-op-Zoom. Tourist offices were not open so the two drove around and chose a hotel by sight, a dark, small, inexpensive looking one across the street from the railroad station. "It had a pool table in the front room," Kit wrote. "They all do."

They got lucky. Their room included twin cots, twin sinks, lots of blankets and breakfast. It cost $3.00 for the two of them. After settling into their room and eating a small supper from their provisions, the girls headed out in search of coffee and a cookie. Rusty described their expedition in a letter to her mother:

> *The streets were loaded with cute Dutch soldiers. Girls were a curiosity enough on that street, but Americans (and they must smell us, because they always know!) – They were very nice – but we caught many little murmurs, low whistles, wide grins, etc. – They're all so big – so rangy looking – and what wide grins everyone had. — and the <u>rosy</u> <u>cheeks</u>!!! We finally got our coffee (koffie) and cookie in small café, and the radio was playing loudly – We heard all kinds of American songs sung in Dutch and played by a Dutch orchestra. – Sounded so gay – so perfect.* —Rusty

The next morning they found that breakfast was more generous than what they had been getting. Rusty wrote home:

> *Up to now every breakfast has consisted of buns and coffee - nothing more, because neither the French nor the Belgium people have anything else – but Holland is a fat healthy country. – so we had slices of cheese, 3 kinds of sliced cold meat, soft-boiled egg, huge*

chunk of butter, luscious strawberry preserves, white bread
(Holland, not like American), funny kind of fruit-sweet bread, and
rusk, — and a pot of coffee. – Also 15% service charge was added on
the bill – ALL this – and only $1.50 each!!! But that was a gem!
They're hard to find! — Rusty

The other big news from Bergen-op-Zoom that they both reported – it was cold! Kit wrote in her journal, "We are freezing to death. Thank God they give you lots of covers." Rusty wrote "But what a COLD night! We nearly froze to death in our room – and nothing is heated!"

Kit bought a pair of shoes in the morning that she had noticed the previous day – a good pair of walking shoes and "for only $3.98!" she happily wrote home. She had seen others before, but they were all $10.00 or more so this was quite a find. In a letter telling her family about this and other experiences in Belgium, Kit noted that the service charge of 15% was either included in the price of the room or added to their bill. "They don't tip anything in Belgium, Holland, or Denmark." she wrote. "In France, of course, they will take as much as you want to throw away but they don't think any better of you for it – in fact, usually less!"

Rusty and Kit departed Bergen-op-Zoom around 10:30 a.m. on September 24 and set off for Rotterdam. In a letter home describing the trip, Rusty wrote:

We drive about 60 when we're on a highway. – and today we were
going 72 – because it was nasty weather and no one was out. –
except cars. – Drove through Rotterdam – the entire center of the
city was blown to pieces in the last war, and it is now all green
grass – The rest of Rotterdam was pretty well blown up too, I guess.
— Rusty

The girls did not stay in Rotterdam but drove on to The Hague, the capital city of South Holland and the seat of the Dutch government and parliament. While in The Hague, they toured the Peace Palace. Funded by Andrew Carnegie, the Peace Palace opened in 1913 to provide an alternate means of conflict resolution and thereby end war between nations.

The girls' young Dutch tour guide took them inside the Peace Palace, through its "beautiful formal gardens" and "a lovely park with winding paths," while describing the history and details of the palace in four different languages. Kit wrote, "It seems as though practically every country in the world donated one or more of the most beautiful things they could find." The Peace Palace received gifts from countries that had participated in the Second Peace Conference held in The Hague in 1907. Gifts included Arabescato marble sent from Italy to decorate the great hall, a double-headed eagle from the Romanovs in Russia, Majolica vases from Hungary, and cloisonné vases from China. While they found the palace both "peaceful and serene," the girls were struck by the irony that construction of the Peace Palace was completed less than a year before the start of World War I.

After their guided tour, the girls left The Hague and drove on to Amsterdam, arriving in the early evening. They checked into the Hotel Park then ate dinner at the Moderne Café in what looked like the "jazzy" section of town.

> *Oh but it was great! We had a Dutch specialty recommended in one of the guidebooks – called "Rolpens." It's a minced beef roll with fried apples on top. With it we had a serving dish full of potatoes – immense salad of lettuce, tomatoes, cucumber and egg – beer and hot chocolate for dessert. All for $1.10!* —Kit

The girls visited the Amsterdam tourist office the next morning to arrange for a less expensive room. At $2.50 each, the large and elegant Hotel Park, which was recommended by someone at the previous hotel, was a bit costly.

> We are getting more and more Scotch _every day_. ...[The] man said 'Fine' – picked up the phone and in one minute we had a room right around the corner from our big hotel for $1.50 each including service and breakfast (with an egg which we didn't get at the first hotel). ...
>
> It was a small place but neat as a pin and we have discovered that the small places give much better service and it's much more fun because you can chat with owner, desk clerk, manager or what have you and learn all kinds of interesting things about the town or country. As soon as you tell these little – interested – people in small type places (as opposed to big, bored people in large-type places) that you are in their country and town for the first time – they love you and knock themselves out recommending special dishes (we have gotten several free desserts, coffee, etc. this way) palaces to go to, etc., and they expect no return for it – they are happy to have you there and all they want is your evident pleasure in their town and native land. We have had many wonderful experiences along this line with people on buses, on the street, - waiters, porters, small hotel managers, tourist offices and so forth. It's a great lesson, and I think a lot of Americans could take a cue from it. —Kit

Having squared away the hotel situation, the girls turned their attention to lunch. They found a place called "The American Lunch Room," and Kit described their very Dutch meal in her journal:

Had a fabulous lunch for $1.50 – just loaded with good food. I had 2 lamb chops, mashed & French-fried potatoes, carrots, string beans, salad, & coffee parfait! Delicious – and a charming looking place – very old-fashioned – a la Luchows only more elegant looking. —Kit

It was another rainy day, but this time the weather didn't stop the girls from getting out and about. After spending time inside writing postcards, Rusty and Kit wandered around and did a bit of shopping. Kit noted in her journal the purchase of a "nylon bra for $.75!" During a visit to the Municipal Museum to see a Van Gogh exhibit, Rusty captured the thrill of being in Europe where so many of the masterpieces were painted:

Went to see a very exciting exhibit of Van Gogh – one of my very favorite artists – And there were many of his pictures there that had been painted in Brussels, The Hague, Paris, etc. — Right where we had been – thrilling, really! —Rusty

According to Rusty, they thought about going out that night, but it was raining, so they gave up and went to bed.

When they awoke, it was still raining. Kit wrote in her journal that it "rained like hell all morning – stayed in and wrote – nearly froze to death." But things brightened up later in the day after a trip to the National Museum (Rijksmuseum) where they were impressed with many paintings by Rembrandt, Vermeer, and de Hooch.

The National Museum has the largest collection of Rembrandts and it too is magnificent. It is really a thrill to see all these famous paintings in their original. They have here the famous – huge – "Night Watch" painting by Rembrandt. It is in an immense room

with rows of benches at the opposite end, to sit and look from. It is very impressive! —Kit

CONCERTGEBOUW - AMSTERDAM

ZONDAG 26 SEPTEMBER 1954 - 2.30 UUR

ABONNEMENTSCONCERT   -   SERIE C Nr 1

HET CONCERTGEBOUWORKEST

Dirigent **Rafael Kubelik**

Solist   **Arthur Rubinstein,** piano

PROGRAMMA

W. A. MOZART 1756-1791	**Symphonie C gr. t., K.V. 338** Allegro vivace Andante di molto Finale. Allegro vivace
ROBERT SCHUMANN 1810-1856	**Concert a kl. t., op. 54** VOOR PIANO EN ORKEST Allegro affettuoso - Andante espressivo - Tempo primo - Allegro molto Intermezzo : Andantino grazioso Allegro vivace

Pauze

ANTONÍN DVOŘÁK 1841-1904	**Serenade E gr. t., op. 22** VOOR STRIJKORKEST Moderato Tempo di Valse Scherzo : Vivace Larghetto Finale : Allegro vivace
HECTOR BERLIOZ 1803-1869	**Ouverture ,,Le carnaval romain", op. 9**

Program for Rubinstein concert.

Kit said Amsterdam was "the place for culture," and after art, it was time for music. The two bought tickets to a concert.

So – at noon – in the rain – we went to see Rembrandt at the museum – And then – very thrilling – we got in to the Concertgebouw Orchestra Concert (They along with the London Philharmonic are the two greatest in the world today!) – and their guest soloist was Rubinstein – rather funny incident happened. –

We got our tickets just as the doors closed, and by the time we had reached the doorway to our particular seats, it was too late and we had to wait till they finished playing Mozart before the ushers would let us in — So we listened and wandered around the halls for awhile and became annoyed because someone was practicing the piano and was drowning out the Mozart — then we realized!! It was Rubinstein himself practicing before he went on! So we hung outside his door and listened to him practice. And then went in to see and watch him play Schussmann with the orchestra which was so beautiful! To be hearing RUBINSTEIN in Amsterdam, Holland — it's too much! My heart may not take all this excitement!!! (ha)
—Rusty

Once they climbed into their $1.10 seats, they found they could hear fine but could not see a thing. During intermission, they enjoyed the local custom of drinking demi-tasse and eating cookies in the lounges for free. Then Kit asked the usher if there was a different place that they could sit where they might be able to see more. She tipped him ten cents (about 50 cents in Dutch money). The usher showed them to center seats in the first row balcony where Kit said they heard the "Serenade in E for Strings" and "Roman Carnival Overture."

Kit and I were reluctant to leave Amsterdam, for that is the first place we have left feeling that it was "unfinished" — There is so much there we didn't see — Mom, — you and I will have to go to Holland in the spring when the tulips are blooming. —Rusty

After the concert, the girls drove on to Leeuwarden, a city in the province of Friesland, and checked into the Hotel Amicitia. In her journal, Kit described it as a "largish hotel — fairly cheap" but lamented that she was "freezing again." Instead of describing the hotel in her letter home, Rusty focused on the driving conditions:

> *The drive there was dark and rainy, — and crossing that <u>long</u> dike was scary!!! The dike was built up too high on our left as we couldn't see the North Sea, but we could see the Zuider Zee, and I kept remembering all my "Dutch" books, etc. – Just unbelievable that <u>I</u> was really <u>there</u>!!!!* —Rusty

The next morning there was sun, and the girls reveled in it. They had missed its warmth and beauty. Rusty wrote, "Holland is a <u>beautiful</u> country!!! Soooo flat! And canals crisscrossing everywhere - Sooo green! And <u>peaceful</u>-looking!"

Amsterdam. It stopped raining! – Rusty

The day was spent driving to Germany with much stopping along the way to take pictures of windmills, canals, and houseboats.

I took one of the darlingest little girl and boy – almost white hair and all in ringlets, — they were about 4 and 5, — and were wearing

Along the road. – Rusty

red sweaters, blue long pants, and red wooden shoes! We just happened to see them along the highway, so we jumped out – the Mother couldn't understand English but she smiled a "Ja!" to the camera – and she's in the picture, too – So cute! —Rusty

They took a small detour to a fishing village on the coast called Delfzjil where they saw men in baggy black corduroy pants and coats, black caps, wooden shoes, smoking big pipes. Kit described lunch on a bluff overlooking the water in a letter home:

Two perfectly fried eggs on HUGE helping of Dutch ham and bread with lettuce and tomato and pickles and yummy hot chocolate. Their ham is the best boiled, sliced type I HAVE EVER eaten! We also took along an apple and some candy for the car. Whole thing cost 75 cents each. They feed you such TREMENDOUS amounts. Did I tell you that after we have finished our trip with all this wonderful food, that we will be walking ads for the old slogan that "Travel is Broadening?" —Kit

On the way back to the main road from their detour, the girls lost their way and flagged down an approaching truck.

Dutch farmer who spoke no English got out – Rusty pointed to the place on the map – sign language and talking in a language the other didn't understand. Then gradually, heads began popping out from all over the truck. Then, one by one, men hopped out. It was like the old little gag in the circus. There were millions of them and not one spoke English! They all talked and pointed like mad. Rusty gave up – nodded her head and said "OK." They piled in and drove madly away – waving and grinning immense Dutch grins (and they ARE immense, believe me!). —Kit

No sooner had the Dutch truck driven off and the girls gotten back in the car than Kit backed them into a ditch!

The flat Dutch countryside stretched for miles and not a soul around. ... It was then about 6:30 – getting darkish – because of clouds and slight drizzle. Needless to say – we got the giggles – then we made one final effort with me pushing – AND WE MADE IT! —Kit

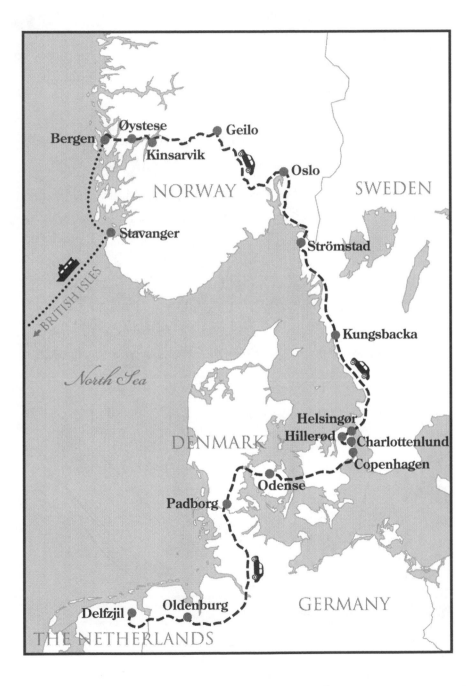

Scandinavia

*Am beginning to think America has
very dull food on the whole. We have
become the "productionized" – quantity –
cheap and quick.*

~Rusty Tyler

10

Glimpsing Germany
(September 27, 1954)

Rusty and Kit continued north from The Netherlands toward the Scandinavian kingdoms of Denmark, Sweden, and Norway, curving across only the intervening portion of Germany. As the girls neared the German border and German customs, they heard an ominous muffled thud.

> *Rusty gasped — we looked down and the top had come off our ¾ full bottle of red wine as it fell over. Wine was sloshing all around the floor of the car. Again by the side of the road - just stood and looked at it, horrified. Finally remembered our roll of toilet paper in the back seat — and we kneeled by the side of the road - madly mopping up pungent, red wine with miles and miles of T.P. What a sight!*
> —Kit

Although the car must have reeked of red wine, the girls had no trouble at the borders.

Dutch customs zoomed by and then we rode into the <u>German</u> customs. It was about 6:00 PM and getting dark, — and suddenly out popped a German officer that scowled, and I could just see him goose-stepping and crying "Heil Hitler." (This was the most exciting one we've been through yet.) He directed me with brittle quick movements and many scowls where to park. — And then we sat and waited about 15 min. – expecting the worst. – but all the rest of the German customs men were most pleasant and this one turned out to be a snap, too! We either look too poor to try and bring money and liquor in illegally, or else too dumb, — or else we have very innocent faces, — because there is a limit on how much money you can take into each country, and we haven't even been asked yet!! —Rusty

Their first stop on the way to Denmark was Oldenburg, Germany. Rusty and Kit had trouble finding a room for the night but eventually found one at the Hotel Fischer. Kit was happy to note, "It was actually warm in our room! Wow!"

With plans to explore more of Germany later in the trip, the following day they continued northward, beyond Oldenburg to Germany's border with Denmark.

Stopped for a bite to eat at roadside type place – WEIRD! Dark, grubby, several women around – grandmother, daughter, granddaughter it looked like. Didn't speak word of English. Place very grubby. Ate in front room which had several tables, they ate family style there too. Had greasy pork chop and immense helping of vinegary potato salad – awful but interesting. —Kit

The weather was dreary as they drove. Both Kit and Rusty noted in their correspondence that the German countryside was much different than that of The Netherlands. The Netherlands had been quite flat and open. In this part of Germany, they found hills and pine forests. With poignancy, they later wrote of the scars of war.

> *Bremen and Hamburg (both are big industrial cities) were very depressing, we thought. Although we saw <u>many</u> new modern bldgs., still, there were so many shells of bldgs., — huge vacant lots still containing rubble, — And evident marks of the War – Marks that we had left, — homes we had bombed! – And along with a gray drizzly rain it wasn't a cheery sight.* —Rusty

11

Dining in Denmark
(September 28 - October 2, 1954)

Rusty and Kit completed the drive through Germany and crossed the border into Denmark around 8 p.m. They had no reservations but found an "adorable" place to sleep in the border town of Padborg. Kit described the room as "very Scandinavian – all white inside with darling little wall decorations – plants all around – copper pots and WARM!" Rusty wrote home, at length, about the supper they had there that night:

We had a delightful meal to "thaw us out"- Must tell you about it! We needed something very hot, - so we looked [on the menu] under the soups – and decided on bouillon with egg thinking that would be something like Chinese egg drop soup – hmmm – you should have seen our eyes when the pretty blonde Danish waitress brought us huge bowls of steaming bouillon and then set down a small glass dish filled with course salt in which sat two half egg shells with a

*raw egg-yolk in each. We looked at that, - at each other, - and tried
to subdue our giggles. ... We didn't know what to do, and finally
decided it was better to show our ignorance and ask, rather than
blunder. - Kit used the sign-language again and the waitress
smilingly, said, "Ja!" – So – we each took our egg shell and bravely
slipped the egg yolk into our soup —stirred it around with our
spoon - and it was delicious! The soup was so hot it cooked it!!! And
it was lots of fun, really.*

*Then we had smørrebrød (ø in Danish is pronounced something like
"or") which Denmark is famous for. It means sandwich, and some
cafés in Copenhagen had 179 (and more) varieties!! They are all
open-faced – and the most delicious things I've ever tasted!
Americans, I've decided, are very foolish to put a slice of bread on
top – it kills the flavor of the filling! We had several varieties in
Denmark:*

*Roast beef and well-browned onions on slice of dark dark bread with
a fried egg on top – <u>MAGNIFICENT</u> – My favorite.*

*Ham on rye, and a scoop of vegetable mayonnaise salad and a curly
cucumber slice on top.*

<u>Dark</u> bread with <u>curry</u> salad and oodles of mushrooms!

and others –
—Rusty

Rusty found the presentation of food and the restaurant service
superior to what was customary in America.

*Another thing we have noticed, is the <u>service</u> you get in restaurants
in all of Europe. – It far surpasses American service!!! For instance:
<u>Always</u> – linen tablecloths, - no matter how cheap the restaurant is.*

And even in the cheapest class of cafés, the waiters are dignified, very pleasant, and with each thing they set down for you they say the equivalent of "if you please – ." <u>Nothing</u> is <u>ever</u> <u>slung</u> at you the way it <u>many</u> <u>times</u> is in America!!!

Really, the service and atmosphere is always so pleasant! We find ourselves eating slower and slower and slower – It's wonderful! Soo relaxing! And I'm liking so many of the ways they serve things – am making many notes and am going to alter my ways when I get home – will serve European style – I love it! Such as:

<u>Everywhere</u> the soup is served in a big <u>tureen</u>. The waiter with a large ladle, dishes you up a large (as big or bigger than the soup bowls we used to have out home) soup bowl full; then walks away leaving this large tureen and soup ladle at your table. To get our money's worth, Kit and I always <u>finish</u> the soup! And <u>every time</u> we have each had <u>three</u> bowls full! So we have discovered we can very cheaply have a meal of soup.

Coffee is <u>always</u> served in a coffee pot; and the cups are <u>always</u> demitasse size. That goes even for Scandinavia where their coffee tastes about the same as American coffee. The coffee pot is either pottery that matches the cup and saucer, or else it's silver. And we each can <u>always</u> have at least 3 cups; and we <u>have</u> gotten as many as 5 cups each! I guess 3 demitasse cups would make about 1½ of our coffee cups. And sugar lumps are in a small silver or pottery dish; and the creamers are tiny and always individual. Also, I haven't used a teaspoon (or <u>seen</u> one) since we left the Queen Mary. Soup spoons are regular tablespoons to us, and all other spoons (for dessert, coffee, tea, - anything) are demitasse size. I had once decided I didn't want the demitasse cups and spoons, but I have now changed my mind. I love them! So much more elegant and gracious *somehow. And you can sit over coffee anywhere as long as you wish. No one ever hurries you out. - No one ever seems to rush, and it's wonderful!!*

Your dinner is always brought in on a platter. Usually the meat … is in the middle and the vegetables arranged very artistically around it. Then the waiter serves you portions on your plate; and the platter containing the remainder is often times placed on a silver box that has 2 candles inside, at your table. This keeps it hot and you can help yourself whenever you want more.

Dessert is served (cookies, cake, pastry, - etc.) … and you help yourself. – Serve it onto your plate. –

Kit has cheese and crackers often for dessert, and she is usually served a saucer with crackers, and many times they will then bring in a huge wooden circular platter containing big wedges of about 8 different kinds of cheese. She chooses the one she wants, and the waiter cuts off a big piece and puts it on her plate.

And so on and on and on – one could write a book just about eating in Europe! And we haven't been in any of the expensive restaurants either!

Also one could write a BOOK on the bathrooms or toilets in Europe. Sometime I'll write you a letter on them!

(I'm watching the weight, tho – don't worry!)

You would love the bread over here! Each country is different – and each has so much flavor and texture.

Am beginning to think America has very dull food on the whole. We have become the "productionized" – quantity – cheap and quick -

Everyone says English food is very tasteless, too – well – we'll see –

Here's Kit – must leave –

More later –
—Rusty

The girls started out the next morning and headed towards Copenhagen. Along the way they lunched in Odense.

Had marvelous thing – steak (flank I think) flopped in half with chopped onions, mushrooms and mustard sauce in between. Served with lettuce and tomato, parsley potatoes, French fries (more like crisp brown potato chips), string beans. Whole thing was marvelous! Including tip and milk - $1.00. —Kit

Rusty added that after lunch, while their car was getting an oil change and they were strolling around the streets of Odense, "two darling little boys (about 9 or 10) asked us for our autographs!!! We got a big charge out of that!"

The girls had to take a short ferry ride across Strebælt (a strait between the Danish islands of Zealand and Funen) to get to Copenhagen since at the time there was no bridge. Rusty described the view from the ferry, "The sun came out for about ½ hour (5:00 PM) and the rainbows and rosy clouds and white sailboats and small fishing schooners, and a far away white lighthouse – lovely!"

Rusty noticed as they drove through Denmark that it seemed people were staring at them more than before. She offered two ideas about this: 1) The Renault was now more unusual as most of the cars on the road around them were American or Volkswagen (German); or 2) There were fewer women drivers.

Rusty recounted their late arrival in Copenhagen:

Drove into Copenhagen in pouring rain. And Charles [her mother's friend and later her husband] didn't want to drive in Salt Lake at night! Ask him how he'd like to drive into a city of over a million population, in the rain, in a country where you don't know the language, and where the road signs, stop and go lights, and policemen's signals are all different, — ?????? It doesn't bother me or at least it hasn't so far – We just drive around and around – terribly lucky! We had heard the Mission Hotels were very good, and so stopped near an outdoor phone booth, and Kit dashed in to copy down addresses of the various Mission Hotels. – But of course the streets were Greek to us! And it was raining! So we drove around a couple of blocks – and Kit happened to glance down a side street and notice 2 Hotel signs, — so I turned around and we went back, deciding we'd better take anything that nite and look for a Mission Hotel the next day. – Lo and behold we looked up and there was HEBRON MISSION HOTEL! Nice, clean, — very plain but more than adequate! 75 cents a day! And that's the way things have been happening to us – We're just plain lucky!!! —Rusty

Kit wrote to her parents what Rusty did not, that they were in search of a service station as well as a hotel:

Car had developed a terrible noise in rear where Rusty banged into tree this morning so we were looking for a service station. —Kit

"Crummy weather still. About ready to give up on it!" summed up Kit in her journal on her first morning in Copenhagen. The girls ventured out nevertheless to go shopping and take in the Permanent Exhibition which featured handmade Danish wares.

They also tried, unsuccessfully, to get ballet tickets – "Damn!" wrote Kit.

They stopped for coffee at a café opposite the Royal Theatre named Café a Porta, one of the famous literary cafés of Copenhagen. Hans Christian Andersen lived on the second floor of the building from 1866 to 1869 and was a frequent patron of the café.

> *And this sidewalk café has infra red lights along the edge of the awnings, and blankets are given to you to put around your legs. Later on in the year, the waiter told us they have a tiny stove containing hot coals for each table, for the people to put their feet on. – And they keep the sidewalk café open until the day before Christmas! Such fun! Everyone all bundled up and sipping hot coffee outside – I loved it!!!* —Rusty

Then Rusty continued on to describe some of the many "small world" situations she seemed prone to experiencing:

> *At breakfast in our first hotel in Amsterdam we met a boy that had been on the Queen Mary with us! He had gotten off at Cherbourg, too, – Nice, but then we left that hotel right way because it was too expensive.*

> *We chatted with a German boy who spoke excellent English while we were on a tour together through the Peace Palace at The Hague. – Then – 2 days later we were just coming out of the Rijk museum in Amsterdam and we met him coming in! Chatted for a second –*

> *Kit and I were on the second floor of the Exhibit, when who should walk up and grab our arms but Dan, – one of the 3 American boys on the Queen Mary. Remember, I told of a party we went to in their cabin? He and the other 2 boys (all graduated from Michigan State*

in '52) had docked in Southampton, England, had toured London and environs for a week; — then went to Paris, bought a Renault, drove up through Belgium and Holland and here we were bumping into each other on a 2nd floor of a store in <u>Copenhagen</u>! — <u>But</u> we also discovered that we were staying in the <u>same</u> <u>hotel</u>, and their black Renault was the one I had parked next to the night before! <u>Now</u>, isn't that a coincidence? So that night after dinner we, all five, went out together for a long talk about our European experiences. —Rusty

The weather continued to be cold and rainy the following day. The girls did some more shopping, and Kit bought a "clothespin apron" which she planned to embroider for her mother.

In the evening they drove to Charlottenlund to visit a friend of Rusty's – Mary Krabbe. Rusty and Mary were in the same sorority at Northwestern University, and Rusty had received a card from Mary saying she would be in Copenhagen soon staying at the home of her aunt and uncle. Rusty wrote home about the visit:

Anyway we had a very nice chat and pleasant evening. And the funniest thing! At 9:30 the Krabbes had to listen to "Mr. Gregory," a mystery program on the radio! <u>Nothing</u> could ever make them miss it! And they told us that it is the only <u>continuous</u> (serial) program on their radio, and that the entire country of Denmark is listening to it! The Govt. owns the radio system —<u>and</u> at 9:30 PM on Friday nights, the <u>movies</u> are stopped, <u>plays</u> are stopped – everything ceases, and the theatres amplify their radio set – and everyone listens to "Mr. Gregory!" We laughed and laughed and laughed over it! Then we listened to about 5 min. of it – all in Danish so of course we couldn't understand it, but the sound effects, music, etc. sounded typically <u>mysteryish</u>!!! —Rusty

The Krabbes persuaded Rusty and Kit to find a room in Hillerød (which they did at the Hotel Leidersdorff) that night so that they could see two castles the following day – Frederiksborg Castle, which was in Hillerød, and Kronborg Castle, which was in Helsingør (also known as Elsinore in English). Frederiksborg Castle was home to many Danish Kings. Kronborg Castle was the setting for Shakespeare's "Hamlet." In the play, the castle is called Elsinore.

Rusty and Kit were intrigued with the two castles and compared them to each other (Kronborg was the typical "cold and empty" variety and Frederiksborg was "warm and cozily furnished") and to other castles they had seen.

> *The Danes keep their things so well! Everything was in perfect condition!!! — so different from the French! And we kept remarking about the contrast between Frederiksborg Castle, the home of the King and Queen of Denmark in the 17th and 18th century, and Versailles, the home of the King and Queen of France in the 17th and 18th century. Versailles is immense, elegant, beautiful, and cold. The Danish castle was very large, lovely, ornate, but warm.* —Rusty

The girls continued to work their charm on men they encountered. In fact, without even asking, they received a private tour of Frederiksborg Castle from one of the museum guards.

> *We met a very cute little Danish guard in the Queen's chambers. He couldn't speak English, but held up a rope barring entrance to one section of rooms and motioned us to duck under. Then he took us to a room full of the Queen's trinkets, and he wound up a birdcage – and it began to sing – sounding just like birds!! Inside the cage were two stuffed birds which then began to move slightly (looking very real), and the bottom of this gilt cage was a clock, —*

keeping perfect time! Then he proudly escorted us through a few
other rooms, now and then stopping to play a music-<u>clock</u> –
<u>beautiful</u>! No music box I ever heard before sounded like this!!
—Rusty

From Frederiksborg Castle they drove on to Kronborg Castle. Rusty, with her theater background, loved Shakespeare, and was greatly affected by seeing "Hamlet's castle." She wrote to her mother:

Then we came to Helsingør, or "<u>Elsinore</u>" in <u>Hamlet</u>. And we drove
out to Kronborg Castle which is the castle that Shakespeare used as
the castle for Hamlet!!! I think seeing this gave me one of the biggest
thrills I've had since I came to Europe. I certainly didn't expect it to
affect me like this, — but – it was so terribly impressive and so
exactly the way Shakespeare wrote of it. We walked across the moat
and looked up at the tall stone walls with wings of grass growing at
the top and kind of sticking over, — and little tufts of grass growing
out of the cracks in the wall. Tiny barred (old and crumbling)
windows, like dark suspicious eyes, looked out of the wall.
Fascinating and formidable, the castle stood, as we looked up at the
many stone towers; and high on the peak of the highest one, a golden
weather vane caught the sun and blazed against the blue sky – We
went inside into the stone courtyard – What a <u>different</u> castle from
the one at Hillerød. This was the castle of – moody, cold, the scene of
unhappiness and secrets. – We climbed to the stone parapets which
overlooked the sea. I was caught almost like in a spell. The wind
rustled the grass, the sea slapped gently at the rocks below and I
could hear so terribly plainly, "To be or not to be. … " … It seemed
the castle was built just for Hamlet and for Shakespeare to write
about. Kit and I didn't <u>want</u> to know what king built it, and who

had <u>really</u> lived there; it would have spoiled it – Hamlet and Ophelia and Gertrude and Pelonius and the rest seemed so <u>real</u>!!! We saw the winding stone staircases, the cobblestone passageways, and I

Me – Elsinore Castle. – Rusty

heard the cannon as they carried Hamlet along these very halls and stairs – Ghosts of the play were everywhere! – Kit and I walked all around it – it's built on almost an island in the sea, and we could see the land of <u>Sweden</u> on the other side. —Rusty

12

Touring Through Sweden
(October 2 – October 4, 1954)

In order to get to Sweden, Rusty and Kit took a short ferry from Helsingør to Helsingborg, Sweden. Upon arrival, they proceeded through customs, where they received a sticker for their windshield reminding them to drive on the left hand side of the road! Rusty wrote home to her mother about this challenge:

> At first I was scared kind of, but I soon got used to it and it bothered me only when someone _passed_ me. To suddenly have a car come whizzing around on my right always startled me. Otherwise, — even in cities, such as Gothenburg, I was fine. – In practice for Great Britain. (ha!) —Rusty

Kit also mentioned driving on the wrong side of the road but kept it brief in a postcard she sent to her parents. "Keep your fingers crossed!" she wrote.

Rusty was impressed with the Swedish countryside, finding it more beautiful than she imagined. She noted, "Everything suddenly was much bigger (after being used to Belgium, Holland, and Denmark) – the farms were further apart, the houses were bigger. And so were the people! – (ha)." They stayed in Kungsbacka, Sweden, for the night.

The next morning they were dealt a small setback. Kit chronicled this adventure in a letter home:

> Got up next morning and went out to the car and – EUROPA
> WOULDN'T START! We were petrified! Couldn't imagine what
> was wrong. We were also in a very small town. Frantically dug the
> Shell book Bud gave me out of the glove compartment – leafed
> through and found a phrase which said, "My car won't start." in 12
> different languages, including Serbo – Croat and Arabic. Ran down
> the road to a gas station, pointed to phrase in book – young man
> chuckled said "Ja, ja" and motioned for us to go back to the hotel
> and wait. (Our sign language is getting excellent!) We did so.
> About 20 minutes later, young man pedaled up on bicycle. We eyed
> each other dubiously. He babbled in Swedish. We in English. Then
> hotel manager appeared – "yes, the young man [is] the mechanic" to
> us and "Yes, these were the young ladies with the car that wouldn't
> start" to him. Off to the garage to look at Europa. Young man
> didn't seem to have any tools with him and a Renault is a Ford car,
> so we were definitely scared – and, of course, he didn't speak
> English. But he seemed to know where everything was. He fiddled
> around and the hotel man and he kept jabbering in Swedish. We
> kept asking hotel man what they were saying but I don't think his
> English was too good. Probably limited to hotel terms and not
> engines – so he would laugh and shrug his shoulders. Then
> suddenly, the engine roared – young man madly tightened bolts and

things and it was done! We gave him 10 kroner – about $1.75 and
practically threw our arms about him. He looked leery – jumped on
his bicycle and pedaled away vigorously. —Kit

Once the car was running again, the girls continued driving
through Sweden on their way to Norway, which they expected to
reach the following day. Kit wrote in her journal about the
Swedish countryside:

Drove all day – weather started out pretty but clouded up – scenery
in Sweden is magnificent! Never saw anything like it before – it got
more and more mountainous as we drove north – winding roads up
and over and down the mountains –immense dark green pine trees
thick all over them with shades of brown and yellow from the
turning birches. It is a beautiful contrast both color-wise and form-
wise – The firs are so sturdy and straight while the birches are
delicate – bending and with leaves shivering and shaking constantly
… Then there are the millions of lakes and rivers everywhere – we
were constantly gasping at the breathtaking beauty. The farms are
very neat – beautifully laid out and very prosperous looking.
Stopped at a little café on the highway and had delicious local cheese
sandwiches, a pitcher of milk – (3 full glasses each), yummy cream
cake and coffee.

Staying at adorable hotel in Strömstad. Sitting downstairs in front
of little roundish burning fireplace. Town is lovely – situated on a
pretty harbor. —Kit

13

Cascading in Norway
(October 4 – October 11, 1954)

Rusty and Kit did not spend long in Sweden; after one night, they set off for Oslo, Norway. Rusty wrote her mother about the drive:

> *Early Monday we suddenly came to a huge bridge spanning a deep gorge into the earth, — rushing clear water a long way down! — an inlet which we discovered divided Sweden and Norway. – Across the bridge and we returned to the <u>right</u> side of the road! The scenery from there to Oslo was similar but not as pretty somehow. Flatter, and the houses were <u>boxier,</u> and only occasionally did one have a red roof. Gray roofs are so uninteresting! – I have decided I'm going to have a red roof on my house.* —Rusty

Oslo, at first, did not capture their hearts. "Dark and rainy all the time," Rusty wrote. Good shopping was accomplished, however, once they had found their way past the extensive district of medical supplies and long underwear, and the girls found refuge from the rain in a movie theater. Rusty explained:

> *We went to an <u>American</u> <u>movie</u> – "The Quiet Man" – They run at 5:00 at 7:00 and at 9:00. The doors are <u>locked</u> when the movie begins (we tried to go on Monday night but got there at 3 min. to 7:00 and they wouldn't let us in). And you can't sit through it twice. There are different prices for the various seat sections and we had a row and seat number where we had to sit. – No cartoon, no short, no news reel. Just the movie. – It was fun because we were in the midst of all the Norwegian-speaking Norwegians! And the movie was delightful! – and in English! With Norwegian sub-titles! Terribly funny!!! Only "bad" thing was that the audience laughed so heartily, and didn't have to quiet down quickly to catch the next line because they could read it. But because they were laughing and we couldn't read Norwegian we missed several of the funny lines. It was lots of fun, anyway!!! —Rusty*

Kit's journal entry about the next day described some of the shopping in detail but began with a rant about the weather:

> *Horrible! Horrible, Horrible!!! Pouring rain this morning. Rained off and on all day – semi cold too – raw. Had smorgasbord type breakfast only they call it buffet. Ate sardines, ham, soft-boiled egg, several kinds of bread with jam and butter and coffee. Yummy – Rusty had lobster salad! How elegant. Too bad I don't care for it.*

> *Went shopping – Oi Molly! Spent much monies! Could spend thousands more – oh these hand made wooly things. Went completely overboard and bought myself a hand knit ski sweater – it is really sensational – pullover, turtleneck, black, white, gold, blue and red. Cost me about $16.75. A steal at the price I guess but I'll have to live cheap for a long time. Also bought myself pair of black*

wool gloves embroidered with blue and gold. Got gifts too: similar pair of gloves for Toni Berns, and hand knit socks for Joan Daly. Toni's gloves were only about $2.50 and Joan's socks only $1.50.

My eye is getting worse! —Kit

There is no mention of a problem with Kit's eye before this in her journal or any of the letters; however, the next day she decided to seek medical attention, which she later described in her journal:

My eye was <u>horrible</u> this morning – almost shut and there is a little puffy spot on my cheek bone under my eye. Hurts like hell!

Finally went to the Municipal Clinic this afternoon. Very interesting – Doctor really poked at my eye until I was ready to scream! Some sort of an infection. Blepharitis it says on my card. It was awful – then I had to get a penicillin shot. Came back and slept sort of for about an hour – Ate in – cheese, prunes, apricots, carrots, limpa, cookies. Eye doesn't look much different – keep my fingers crossed. —Kit

When Kit awoke the next morning, her eyes were "great" with "no ill effects."

The girls left Oslo at 10 the next morning and drove to Geilo. At the Breidablik Hotel, they found a room and a long glassed-in porch in which to write letters.

Kit and Rusty thought Norway was beautiful. They each invested considerable time writing descriptions of the countryside. Kit wrote in her journal on October 7:

Norway is the most magnificent and breathtaking country we have seen so far. The firs are tall, dark and sturdy and the birches with their silver white trunks are delicate with shimmering sunny leaves which tremble at the slightest whisper of a breeze. Then there are light yellow and bright red maples which line the road and grow in the still lush green pastures in the many fertile valleys. Every corner you turn provides a more fresh and beautiful combination of colors than before. We drove through sections which were nothing but solid birch trees – it was like driving through a tunnel of bright sunshine. —Kit

Rusty wrote home about their drive from Oslo:

The highway was small and winding, and after only about 50 kilometers it turned into a dirt road. ... Rounding another curve we gasped as we beheld a panorama suddenly spreading out before us: - mountains rising out of mirror-like water, tiny islands dotting the large "fingered" lake; red barns and yellow houses hugging the sides of the mountains, peaking between the trees, and nestling in a tiny valley near the edge of the water. ... We stopped beside a waterfall, in the midst of this Technicolor world and had our lunch of Norwegian cheese, Swedish limpa bread (you'd love it! It's dark dark *brown, and a wonderful unique flavor with a very few raisins here and there), tomatoes, raw carrots, dried prunes and apricots and Swedish cookies (similar to your pepper-pots). ... For nearly 200 kilometers we followed along the edge of a wide clear river which at every other turn widened out into a "lake"... Kit and I stopped again beside the road and clambered up and down rocks, tramped through thick woods, and picked a few leaves to show you some of the colors that filled our world this afternoon. ... We stopped for a hot cup of coffee in a small roadside inn; - and suddenly back in the car and driving I glanced down, and the tiny field I saw was spotted with snow!!! Soon, it was all about us, and then the road became slushy with graying snow.* —Rusty

After a smorgasbord breakfast at the hotel in Geilo the next morning, Rusty wrote, "Kit and I dashed out in the fresh cold snowy winter's morning and took a picture of each other in our ski sweaters with Norway in the background! Then we warmed up Europa and started on our way!"

Rusty wearing the sweater she purchased in Oslo.

Before they began their journey over the mountain on the way to Bergen, the girls stopped at a gas station. While the attendant refueled the car, they scrutinized the map. Rusty wrote:

... The tourist man in Oslo had told us to inquire about the roads and the weather; - so we have, and they say the roads between here and Bergen are still open. From the 1ˢᵗ of October on, they may be closed at any time. ... —Rusty

But when the attendant noticed where they were pointing to on the map, he began to speak rapidly and with some urgency, tapping on the map to try to get his point across. Unfortunately, he spoke no English, and the girls did not speak Norwegian. They could not understand what he was trying to tell them and in the end "fluffed it off," as Kit said, and away they went:

Left Geilo about 10:00. Drove about 15 minutes thru same terrain as late yesterday afternoon. Then as we climbed the trees disappeared, then the bushes and we were alone on a road covered with snow with nothing but huge brown rocks, bright white snow and misty clouds around us. Road was steep at first and very slippery – filled with half frozen slush. We would crawl around a curve – slip a little and then glance to the left and see nothing next to us but a sheer drop of a thousand feet or more. Looking up we could see nothing but high snowy mountain tops with angry looking gray clouds sitting on them. —Kit

As they drove, Rusty was surprised by the roads.

There were slim poles on either side of the road, all the way – about 15 feet high and 20 feet apart. – They were for the snow plows – so they can tell where the road is! And we passed a snow fence which was about 20 feet <u>high</u>, and hung about half way up, were deer-<u>hides</u>. The fence must have been nearly a quarter of a mile long, and the hides were close together all the way! Wish we had counted them! —Rusty

Kit continued in her journal:

Climbed and climbed and each time the grade would become more gradual then flatten out a little to look as we had come to the top – we would go over a little rise and there would be another long slope before us. This went on for almost 2 hours. Drove in second [gear] nearly the whole time at about 20-30 kilometers. Passed nothing but dark gray mountain lakes, streams and an occasional summer hunting lodge-boarded up for winter. Had no idea how long it would last. Seemed endless – a wasteland. Beautiful blue mountains in the distance. Then began descending gradually – snow got less and less, brown grass began poking thru – now and then a house. Our wasteland was behind us – Now a strange and eerie world began unfolding. Everything a crazy rusty brown. Huge mountains still all around – some snow-capped. Coarse reddish creeper all over – low stump trees, gnarled birches. Drifting through the crevasses and hanging over lakes and trees shreds of mist. Brown and red got richer – then fertile green valley. Then … Huge gorge – biggest most amazing thing I have ever seen – rushing river tumbling over immense boulders thousands of feet down to the bottom – drove round and round to bottom – gorgeously fantastic. Know now where Greig [Norwegian composer & pianist] got his inspiration. Took ¾ of an hour to get to bottom – Then drove along lovely valley to a fjord which we followed to Kinsarvik. Emotionally exhausted by this time – what a day! Took ferry over to Kvanndal then drove here to Øystese, Bergen tomorrow. —Kit

Rusty emphasized the beauty instead of the danger in her descriptions of their perilous trip over the mountains:

Not a sign of anyone anywhere!! … I stopped once to take a picture, and stepped into snow only 2 feet from the car (in the road) that went way above my ankle! We high-centered on snow in the middle of the road often. – Then in this world of gray and white we noticed rich blue mountains ahead – and suddenly we saw that we were driving toward a deep blue mountain, flanked by white mountains, and in the "pocket" we saw white steam boiling up. Eerie! Within half an hour we approached it and then started our decline – down a rocky road leading into this rolling frothing steam. I felt we must be

A portion of the treacherous route from Oslo to Bergen.

surely driving down to Hades – Everything was so weird – nothing seemed real – And that Kit and I were driving in a little car in this mysterious country seemed completely unbelievable!!!

The snow became thinner and thinner as down down down we went – suddenly the steam was swirling above us and we were in a land of gnarled and twisted birch trees (not the tall graceful ones of yesterday) – The leaves and all the grass and bushes were rust colored. It looked liked everything had been thoroughly wetted and then had corroded and rusted. And the land was rocky and rough Soon other colors became visible. We noticed a deep rich red leafed plant growing close to the earth, and golden tinges and a faint green here appeared about us. And then we gasped!! The most beautiful sight you have ever seen! We were plunging down into a chasm — sheer rocky cliffs and high rock mountains all about us – Mountain streams tearing madly over the rocks – Rusty iron rocks – Black and burnt orange – small bits of red plants and olive green grass growing bravely here and there.

The road wound and dropped down unendlessly – it seemed we were going down into the very bowels of the earth. Steamy clouds swirled up and above us – Trees, gold and orange, appeared, stubbornly clinging to the mountains – Down down down. – it seemed there was no bottom! All the snow was gone – We stopped once, and clambered up on mossy green rocks; — a waterfall in front of us, tearing and rushing down and between huge rocks – sheer rock precipices on either side, high above us – clouds swirling around the top, — Beautiful and frightening! On the other side of the road we looked down on another waterfall far below us – and more rocky mountains high above. The ruggedness, wildness, beauty — strange and weird is impossible to describe – Only by seeing could you believe! And we continued to go down – along rocky cliffs, over tiny natural rock bridges, through long inky-black rock tunnels from which water dripped in large and ominous drops. – As we neared a leveling-off-place, a few sheep began to peer at us – black ones and white ones — very large ones. (The descent lasted 45 minutes, so you can imagine how far down we really were going!) Golden birches, red maples, and green pines again appeared in beautiful array - but our road continued around rocky mountains and soon *we discovered we were coming out of the canyon and were driving along a fjord! The mountains are all rock, it seems, and the road twists along on the side of them, — Straight down is the beautiful inky black water of the fjord. Norway is a beautiful country! Gigantic, massive, rugged, and gorgeous!* —Rusty

After the 120-kilometer harrowing drive from Geilo, the girls stopped in Kinsarvik for hot soup and hot coffee, then drove aboard a "tiny little ferry" and started on an hour's journey along a fjord to Kvandall. According to Rusty, "The fjord trip was lovely but foggy and impossible to take a single picture – Also very cold."

The girls spent the night in Øystese, which Kit described as a "pretty little town." In a letter home to her parents, she explained its pronunciation – "something like 'oyster' the way Uncle Bill would pronounce it." Uncle Bill was from Baltimore, Maryland.

Rusty and Kit's goal for the next day was to reach Bergen, Norway, and board the boat that would take them and Europa across the North Sea to England. They arrived in Bergen in the early afternoon. The drive was pretty, but also rainy and windy, which made it a bit stressful, as Rusty described in a letter home:

Through winding mountain passes, down gorges, through tiny villages, up narrow roads, looking straight down to waterfalls and tiny far-away valleys; — through long rock tunnels that dripped water, — round and round, up and down – Pretty, but a strain when it was raining. Kit did your share of "frightened noise-making"! – (ha!) —Rusty

The first thing they did when they got into Bergen was check-in at the Berg-Hanson Line office to make sure all was confirmed with their ferry reservation. They were asked where they had come from, and the girls replied "Geilo." The clerk was quite surprised and asked them more about their route. He called other staff over and all agreed that it was quite impossible because that road over the mountain was closed! Now it seemed clear what the man at the gas station must have been trying to tell them. Kit elected not to include this bit of information in a letter home. She only included the following about checking in at the ferry office:

Europa and Kit – between Geilo and Øystese. – Rusty

Met a wonderful little man who told us all about the boat and what kind of crossing he thought we might have. Told us what we had already heard many times – that the North Sea is the roughest crossing there is usually. Also told us about the Danish freighter which had gone down a couple of days before – but, said we had nothing to worry about and so we went away much cheered (???).
—Kit

The girls were not allowed to board the boat until 8 p.m. so they had a leisurely lunch and planned to poke around the shops the rest of the time. Their timing was a little off, however. Kit told the tale in a letter home:

> *I was reading the little guidebook the steamship man had given us and discovered to our horror that the stores all closed at 3:30 p.m.! It was then 3:15. Frantically checked the movies – none started until 7:00 p.m. Museums all close at 3:00 after October 1st. We had <u>no</u> <u>place</u> to go! Weather was worse – two little waifs – we finally looked up the three best hotels in our guidebook and figured we would go and have tea or coffee for an hour and a half in each one – or just sit if we could get away with it. Of course, we both looked like the wrath of the gods from the wind and rain and wrinkled wet coats but off we went. It worked out very well in the first two though we were pretty full of tea after them, but the third looked terribly snazzy – we managed to arrive just as a carload of dinner-dressed men and women were entering so since we were right across from the railroad station, we went to the cafeteria there and had two huge glasses of rich milk for $.06 each and a couple of buns for $.03.*
> —Kit

Rusty continued the description of their day in a letter home. She wrote about boarding the boat:

> *At 8:00 p.m. we drove down to the docks, and were cheered up by very friendly, cute and cheerful Norwegian custom officers! They sat us by a little electric heater to thaw us out, and after we saw Europa being swung into the air on a huge crane and deposited on board the S.S. Leda, — we clambered aboard, too; — and waved goodbye to the custom officers and to Norway as we sailed out of the harbor at 11:00 PM.* —Rusty

The boat, named the *Leda*, could hold about 500 people, though Kit wrote that there were probably only 50 people on board due to the time of year. The fare was much more expensive than the girls anticipated. Although the voyage was only a day and a half, the tickets cost them each $32.50, and food was not included. The trip put a dent in their budget, but Kit also had something else weighing on her mind. She wrote in her journal that night, "[...] worried about crossing. Have a funny feeling."

Because the next stop was in Stavanger, the *Leda* stayed close to shore the first night. Although Kit was worried about getting seasick, the seas were not rough, and both girls felt fine in the morning. Rusty wrote about their day on the boat:

> *The next morning we awoke in our tiny cabin to find we were docked at Stavanger – Dressed quickly and stomped on deck to find the sun shining, a band playing on the dock, and the entire town turned out. – Discovered it wasn't all for us, but rather for a farewell to a Norwegian woman and her two young boys and teenage daughter, who were on their way to New York to join their husband and father. (None of them could speak English.) It was really kind of sad. The girls' school friends were crying, and the band (high school and grade school boys) kept playing. We sailed from there at 11:30 AM; Kit and I were terribly sleepy, so decided to lie down – just for a second. Well, we awoke 2 hours later to find the ship plunging up and down in huge stormy waves. It never bothered me while I was lying down (in fact I kind of enjoyed it; — as I said before it was like lying in a cradle and being rocked) but when we stood up – that was a little different matter – we knew the*

best thing to do was eat, so we made a cheese sandwich (in our cabin) and I had 2 bites then I knew I'd better climb back into bed

Europa being lifted into the cargo hold of the ship.

quick!! But I forced myself to eat the sandwich lying down; — and then ate an apple (tho I felt anything but hungry then.) Kit quickly lay down, too, but she said she couldn't finish her sandwich. And — I felt fine, but she got sicker and sicker and for about 2 hours was in agony and ready to make a dash for the bathroom at any second. — So now I believe even more firmly in eating, — it makes your stomach concentrate on working and not on flying around! I slept and slept and slept! Kit finally felt better, too; — Then about 6:30 we had to get up to go to the bathroom; — and that always made us woozy; — seemed like the ship rocked worst there! So then we decided we had to have a nourishing hot meal; — but the cafeteria didn't open till 7:00 – So, remembering the advice of Bob; — we bundled up and took a long walk on deck. – Exciting!!! The Leda was a very small ship anyway, and those waves were fierce! They rose to nearly the height of the deck! Stormy night – frightening but thrilling — The fresh air helped; — then we went in and had meat and vegetables and I had a glass of milk and took another quick walk on deck – Jumped into bed — The next morning about 6:00 AM we docked. And we felt wonderful!! We had fought valiantly and had won! Kit said she "heard" people on either side of our cabin. I'm glad I didn't — (ha!) —Rusty

In a letter home to her parents, Kit also described the unfortunate, but fairly typical, story of their crossing of the North Sea:

At 1:30 I awoke – got up – took a little walk down the corridor – and by the time I got back to the cabin I thought the world was coming to an end! Fell on my bed – Rusty awoke – got up – same thing. We were dumbfounded. We – the hardy sailors of the Queen Mary – the Dramamine kids – the psychology mind-over-matter gals - ! Well, nothing drastic had happened to us as yet so we decided the best thing to do was eat – got out our bread and cheese – sat on the edge of our bunks and munched a little – worse! Decided we felt best lying down so climbed in and ate lying down – Rusty felt a little better – I felt a little worse – but it was still better lying down. What a lost black day in our lives – we lay all afternoon dozing intermittently and fighting it. About dinner time we awoke and decided to take ourselves in hand – firmly. We were getting headaches from too much sleep. Arose and put on coats and scarves

– went out on deck and marched. It was really wildly beautiful –
scudding white clouds – moon – immense waves which sprayed the
deck – difficult to walk because we were pitching every which way.
At 7:00 we marched grim-faced into the cafeteria – no makeup,
uncombed hair – had our plates piled high with meat and potatoes
and carrots – only about 15 people in the place – very little talk.
Shoveled everything down with determination – spoke not a word –
finished – walked a little more – back to cabin – still not a word –
undressed – fell in bed – blackness … Next morning, Newcastle at
7:30 – got up – felt great! We had pulled through – never got sick.
Oh, I forgot – last thing I remember before I went to sleep was
hearing the woman next door using the large paper cup (they hang
4 large ones on the side of each bunk!) – I think that's why I blacked
*out as quickly as I did! –*Kit

Rusty and Kit (and Europa) disembarked the next morning in
Newcastle, England. They were relieved to be on land again and
in a country where they understood the language. They did not
stay in Newcastle, an industrial city, but headed north
immediately. They were bound for Edinburgh, Scotland.

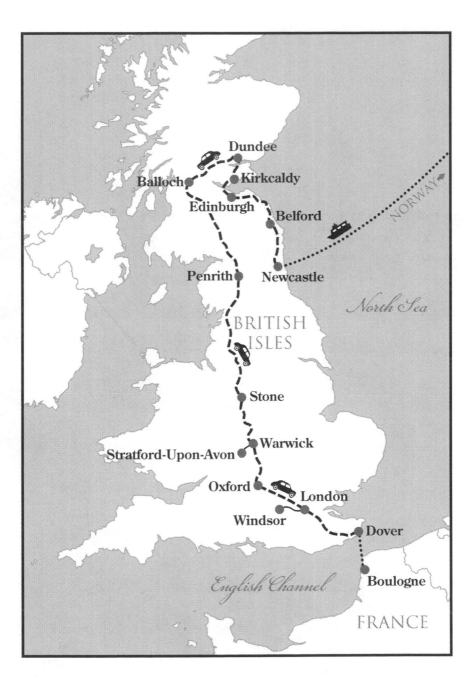

Dundee

Kirkcaldy

Balloch

Edinburgh

Belford

NORWAY

Penrith

Newcastle

North Sea

BRITISH
ISLES

Stone

Warwick

Stratford-Upon-Avon

Oxford

London

Windsor

Dover

English Channel

Boulogne

FRANCE

The British Isles

We walked off the gangplank – to cloudy,
misty gray England.

~Rusty Tyler

14

Climbing Castles in Scotland
(October 11 - October 15, 1954)

"We walked off the gangplank – to cloudy, misty gray England; – with a rigmarole to get through the British customs!" wrote Rusty to her mother.

According to Kit's journal, the two were asked all sorts of questions about the car and their driver's licenses as they went through customs, the worst experience in any country thus far, but this time, they could understand the language. Wrote Kit, "It is really wonderful to be able to understand everything and be able to make yourself understood."

After the rough voyage to England, it was a relief to be on land, and the two girls left depressing, "dull, gray, smoggy, and factoryish" Newcastle and drove north toward Scotland.

The drive was beautiful, and the English countryside was lovely. They saw sheep, green fields, and little stone houses with bright flowers as they drove along the sea. At 12:30, Kit and Rusty stopped at the "darling" and "cozy" Blue Bell Hotel in Belford, Northumberland, where they drank tea and ate cakes in front of a fire before continuing the drive to Edinburgh. Kit wrote to her sister and brother-in-law that it was "just wonderful - like being in someone's front parlor taking tea."

Mid-afternoon on October 11, 1954, the girls arrived in Edinburgh. Kit wrote, "City is lovely, all castles, monuments, and chimney pots." Rusty wrote, "I was thrilled by Edinburgh! It's a beautiful city! – Tall dark spires and castles, and fascinating monuments everywhere!"

> We drove along Princes St. (the main one — notice the postcard) and noticed an _enormous_ crowd of people. We had to drive through it, feeling like we had somehow got in the way of a parade; — and three-quarters of an hour later as we passed near there, an even larger crowd was assembled. We decided they must be waiting for someone to come out of the Royal Hotel, which was across the street; — Bought a paper and sure enough, the Duke of Edinburgh (or "Liz's" husband) had been having some kind of a meeting there. ... Kind of exciting even though we didn't see him. —Rusty

At the tourist office, they chose two of the cheapest and most centrally located hotels, cased them from the outside and chose to go inside one located in a row of houses. Kit wrote, "Never know it was a hotel except for a small sign on railing."

The two wandered into the darkish looking front hall. "Yes?" a young Scottish girl said in a whisper.

> We whispered back that we would like a double room for the night. – she looked dubious then said she would ask if there was one –

disappeared upstairs – more whispering – reappeared – whispered that there was a double room with double bed. ... Climbed upstairs – room was medium-sized, bed was definitely medium-sized – in length and width! Heat was not even medium – it was nil. Looked down and saw an electric heater – happily flicked it on – nothing. Looked closer – one shilling required – didn't have any. Gave up and decided to go outside where it was warm and look at things.
—Kit

After we got our room (in a very small private hotel on Royal Terrace) it was time for tea!... No one on the British Isles would ever dream of missing their tea! And it really is a very nice institution, I think! Would like to incorporate it into America! – Each table is set up with cups and saucers, small plates with a knife on each, pitcher of milk, and sugar; — AND about <u>four</u> or <u>five</u> plates: one contains scones and tiny flat pancakes (sometimes they're potato pancakes); another has Scotch shortbread, another all kinds of fancy cookies, and another has gooey small cakes, éclairs, etc. – The waitress automatically brings a pot of tea and a pot of hot water. And we can order sandwiches and the like, too, but we don't. Then we have 2 or 3 cups of the best tea you've ever tasted; and we've learned that the scones and little pancakes (with their jams and preserves) are delicious, but we leave their sweet things alone. They're much too sweet – dead sweet – And not "heavenly delicious" the way the French and Scandinavian pastries were and you're charged for how much you eat. —Rusty

Kit wrote in a letter to her family, "We had been reading all about teas so ran happily into the first place we found."

Tea is really a fabulous thing – that first one I mentioned was very small – but since then we have really been through some lulu's! Found a real tea place our second day. Lovely restaurant with special room all set up for tea – about 60 tables all set. On each table were several plates – on one there were scones and little pancakes, on another huge currant crumpets, on another several kinds of bread, then a plate of assorted cookies, a plate of assorted pastries and, finally, two huge dark chocolate éclairs. Plus, of course, 3 kinds of jam and sweet butter. We gasped – sat down and ordered a pot of tea – didn't know what to do – if we were supposed to eat everything or what. The waitress wanted to know if we wished eggs and bacon or eggs and chips or anything – we said no and then confessed we didn't know what to do. She kindly explained that you simply ate your way through anything you wanted on the table and when you finished they added up the bill – wonderful system, eh wot? We love it! —Kit

"After tea that first day in Edinburgh we walked up the street, window shopping, looking up at Edinburgh Castle, — high on a rock overlooking the city; — past the Sir Walter Scott Monument," wrote Rusty. According to Kit, the girls stopped in a Howard Johnson-type place for lunch. As they sat there eating hot spicy tomato soup, Rusty suddenly said to Kit, "My heavens, I can understand that woman's newspaper!" After traveling in Europe for a month, finally they were able to understand the language. Kit wrote, "Many nights we have sat and tried vainly to decipher an important looking headline in a strange tongue – a very funny feeling!"

Because Rusty's great grandfather, Archibald Cowan, was a Scot from Dundee, Rusty was intent on finding her family's clan.

Out again into the mist, — past several tartan shops; — AND – outside one, was a huge wooden plaque saying that they could tell you what clan you belong to, — and underneath was this long list of Scotch names. I looked and there was <u>Cowan</u> *– belonging to the Colquhoun clan (pronounced "Cahooan").* —Rusty

On their way back to the hotel, the girls passed a theater and felt they were very much in need of some "night life," so went to two American movies – "Arrowhead" and "Saigon" which Rusty described as "old but good," and Kit described as "crummy."

Back at the hotel, the room was still cold. Kit popped two shillings into the heater but wrote, "It takes quite a while for a little thing like that to have much effect on an old high-ceiling room and though it tried bravely it wasn't terribly successful."

The next morning (gray and cloudy) we had our first breakfast in Great Britain and were we surprised! Listen to this: First we were served hot porridge (very similar to oatmeal) and scones. (All automatically – we're never asked what we'd like.) Then the girl brought us tea and toast. And we nearly flipped when 2 seconds later she put down a plate in front of each of us containing a fried egg, ham, potato pancake, and grilled tomatoes!!!! BREAKFAST! (for 3 days in Scotland we lived on breakfast and tea about 4:00 or 5:00 PM – enough!!!) —Rusty

Enthralled with the castles of Edinburgh, Rusty wrote:

Well fed, we stomped along the Scottish streets to Holyrood Castle, which was gray, somber, but very interesting. Took a 20 minute tour (wonderful little happy Scotsman for a guide – by the way, the people are SCOTS not SCOTCH, we discovered!) through the rooms in which Queen Elizabeth and the Duke live in when they come to Edinburgh! So the next time you see in the newsreels where the Queen and her husband are "relaxing" at Edinburgh, you'll know that I have been there, too!!! Then we explored on our own the ancient private rooms of Mary Queen of Scots. – Her bedroom, "private supping room," dressing room, and the tiny secluded stairs which led to Lord Darnley's bedroom!!! Small, dark, and gloomy rooms, with small barred windows, out of which she must have looked many times! I have had a very close feeling to her ever since my dramatic reading in high school — - — remember?! —Rusty

Next we got Europa and drove up to Edinburgh Castle, which was my favorite and if I were Queen Elizabeth, that's where I'd choose to live when I was in Scotland! It's on the postcard I sent you – built on this huge rock, and built on many levels – Intriguing, fascinating, and ruggedly beautiful!! We walked around the high stone wall, looking down on Edinburgh – a magnificent and beautiful view!!! – into many stone towers, circular staircases, small passageways, etc. – A branch (or something) of the Army of Scotland is quartered in part of the castle; — all of the men, whether in khaki or not, wear the Navy and red Scots caps (like I used to have!). And at the castle we saw many in kilts! (Also saw quite a few men and boys downtown wearing them.) All the guards and guides to the castle (and some of the soldiers) wore Navy blue coats and caps, and their trousers were plaid – and different plaids – evidently denoting their own clan or their division in the Army.
—Rusty

Kit described the castle as immense. She wrote about the several museums within the castle and about the proud Stuart kings and queens and their stubborn Scottish struggles. Both she and Rusty wrote in their letters home about the detail presented in the museum exhibits.

> *In several other rooms of the castle we dreamed over the old relics and museum pieces of the proud Scottish history. Unlike other museums and collection rooms we've been in; — in Scotland they don't have just a collection of pistols, or of costumes, or of dishes, — they have beside each object its entire <u>history</u>. For instance, there were 4 strands of Bonnie Prince Charlie's hair! And beside it was the story of how he had given a lock of his hair to a lady who, when she was dying left it to her son, who in turn gave it as a wedding gift, saying it was the most valuable and dearest thing he possessed. – This then was given to someone else, etc. Until only 4 strands were left and Lady so and such gave this to the castle museum. There was also a bowl that had been glued together and its history was that Bonnie Prince Charlie drank out of it one dark stormy night when he took hidden refuge in the home of a friend. This friend wrenched it from B.P. Charlie, fearing that he was drinking too much and worried about his safety. – In the slight struggle it crashed to the floor and was broken. – And so on and on.* —Rusty

> *We loved the tour guides and the roomkeepers ... They are so proud of their history – you know they have given their spiels over and over again and yet they get such an obvious kick out of doing it still. I was really impressed with the whole thing – the people's attitude towards their history and their background – they are so proud of it and so terribly anxious for you to be interested in it – and we certainly were!* —Kit

As the girls explored the many rooms of the castle, they thought they heard something.

Kit and I thought we were "daft" when we heard bagpipes faintly playing. – The wind was blowing so hard we were nearly blown over many times! – and the howling wind and the bagpipes and this ancient stone castle – quite a combination!! We tried to trace the sound, entered a door marked "private," climbed circular stairs and narrow hall and a locked door – behind which we heard, quite loudly, the bagpipes being played. Stood and listened for a long time and then quietly "sneaked" out —Rusty

The weather was cloudy, drizzly, and windy in Edinburgh, and in spite of the excitement of being in Scotland, Kit wrote in her journal about the city's air quality.

Felt horrible all day! City has constant smog which drives me mad – eyes, throat etc. Really horrible – gets into your lungs – well, you know my throat and sensitive eyes and nose – it was awful – I'm sure I'd be down with TB after two weeks! So far we have found all the large cities – Scotch and English to be this way. Don't know how they stand it! —Kit

"That night we stayed overnight at a little town called Kirkcaldy," wrote Kit, referring to a small coastal town on the East Coast of Scotland about 30 miles north of Edinburgh.

We visited a Scotch couple – friends of Rusty's (sort of). One of their daughters had married a boy from Rusty's home town right after the war and their other daughter went to the States this summer to stay for a year. Their mother went over to visit them in

*South Dakota this past summer and Rusty met her, and Mrs. Smith
insisted that Rusty call her when we got to Scotland.* —Kit

So, the morning of October 12, before the girls went visiting
castles, Rusty called Mrs. Smith. "She seemed so excited and so
anxious for us to come out," wrote Rusty. "Invited us to stay all
night." The girls left Edinburgh about 6:00 p.m. and drove to
South Queensferry.

*While we were going across we met a very nice Scotsman who was
typical of the wonderful genuine friendliness of all the Scots people
and he chattered all the way across about the weather and golf
(which seems to be a national sport of Scotland!) and cars and the
lack of bridges, etc. – and how he trilled those R's! – Then he told us
to follow him and he went out of his way to show us a quick route to
Kirkcaldy.* —Rusty

Because they were hungry, the girls looked for a place to eat
before arriving at the Smiths' but nothing was open. According to
Rusty, "Not one place where you could get a bowl of soup, a
sandwich, ice cream, or <u>even</u> a cup of coffee! And we've found
that every town in Great Britain unless it's a big city like
Edinburgh, is the same way! The towns completely fold up at
6:30! – <u>No</u> <u>good</u>!"

With empty stomachs, they arrived at the Smiths' little house at
about 8:15 p.m. Kit wrote in her journal, "Their house overlooks
an inlet from the North Sea – it's on a cobblestone street which has
a wall all along it – fascinating view."

Soon the girls were sitting in a small and cozy living room
complete with a warm fire, chatting with the Smiths. Kit wrote,

"They were just wonderful – tiny with thick Scotch burrs. … They were so pleased to have us there and we felt right at home."

> *Mr. Smith is as cute as [Mrs. Smith] is – short, but what a build! All man! And he talks with even more of a Scottish "burr" or accent, than she! And <u>loves</u> to talk! The 4 of us had cold meat, scones, cookies, and tea before the fire, and we talked steadily from 8:30 to midnight. Both Kit's and my faces ached from smiling and laughing so much!*

> *They were so cute, and he had a thousand funny stories to tell! We talked about South Dakota a lot; — and Mrs. Smith jumped up once to play a record for me. Guess what it was??!!! Doris Day singing "The Black Hills of Dakota" – It was absolutely impossible for me to believe then that <u>I was in Scotland</u>!!! —Rusty*

Around midnight, the girls went to bed in the Smiths' daughter's room, where Mrs. Smith put hot water bottles in their beds to warm them up. Rusty described the house as:

Mr. and Mrs. Smith - the girls stayed with them in Kirkcaldy, Scotland

Very plain, very simple, but comfortable and it is built high up overlooking the sea!! They have huge windows (a variation of our picture windows) and below are the familiar rock walls, then the docks, and the sea. Far off to the right across the bay and the mouth of the [River] Forth we could see a few outlines of Edinburgh!!
—Rusty

From misty and hilly Scotland, to her mother in dry and flat South Dakota, Rusty wrote:

I can't imagine how Irene [the Smiths' daughter] must have felt, her first few months in Platte [South Dakota]. — Such complete extremes! – in the town, the people, the way of life, — the weather, the atmosphere. You have no idea until you've been there! —Rusty

Mr. Smith returned from his butcher shop to have tea while the girls ate breakfast the next morning. Kit described their second Scottish breakfast. "Hot porridge (oatmeal), fried eggs, hamburger-type cakes, grilled tomatoes, potato pancake, scones and butter and jam, bread, and tea!" Impressed again with the Scottish people, Kit wrote:

Don't let anybody ever tell you the Scotch are a dour difficult people. In all our travels so far they have turned out to be the most helpful, interested, and charming people we have encountered. ... Wherever we were, even buying a piece of candy in a store as soon as it was discovered that we were from out of town, they beamed and wanted to know where we were going, where we had been and if they could help. If you pull over to the side of the road for a second to read your map, in 2 seconds someone is at the car window very politely asking if they can be of assistance. This happened to us many times. They are the most sincerely interested people we have met. If you can't find exactly what you are looking for in one shop,

they consider your problem and then refer you to several other
places with explicit directions on how to get there. If you hesitate at
the price of a hotel room they smile and tell you the hotel across the
bridge is a little less expensive. I could go on for hours, but suffice it
to say – we loved 'em – they are a truly warm and friendly people.
—Kit

Despite the Smiths' invitation to stay, the girls left Kirkcaldy and headed south on October 13. "Left the Smiths' very reluctantly and drove all day through ferocious wind so bad it kept pushing the car around," wrote Kit.

"That day we drove to <u>Dundee,</u>" Rusty wrote. "Don't know why but I had always pictured it as a fairly small rather <u>pastoral</u> town, so was very surprised to find a gray smoky industrial city. We stayed for about an hour. ...."

The girls drove on through Perth and Stirling to Balloch through "terrific rain and wind" where they spent a night at the Tullichewan Hotel in Balloch at the tip of Loch Lomond. On this, their third day in Scotland, Kit wrote about afternoon tea at the hotel:

We succumbed to eggs and bacon and chips (French fries), scones,
crumpets, tiny pancakes with jam, cookies and tea [all for about
$0.55]. You can see how this might eliminate the need for dinner –
especially with one of those breakfasts for ballast from the morning.
Frankly, I don't see how these people manage to stay so lean. Here is
their eating schedule: breakfast – 8:00 – 9:00; "Elevenses" or
morning coffee – 11:00 – 11:30; lunch – 12:30 – 1:30; tea – 2:30 –
5:00 (this starts with "low" tea and ends with "high" tea); dinner –
6:00 – 7:00. And unless you hit them at the listed time, you don't
eat. —Kit

Kit wrote that their room was the coldest they'd slept in so far "without even a shilling-type heater in it. ... Only saving grace was that they put stone-ware hot water bottles in our beds before retiring. That doesn't help your nose any though!"

And the next morning they "drove north several miles along the bonny, bonny banks of Loch Lomond!!! And the sun shone! The first day since Denmark!"

> *But even the sunshine in Britain is misty, took a few pictures, — picked a bunch of <u>heather</u> — and <u>holly</u>! There were shining green holly trees growing all over! And several had bright red berries! So pretty! I didn't know that holly was a tree! I always thought it was a bush! — Kit and I lustily sang "Oh ye'll take the high road, and I'll take the low road. ... " and "Annie Laurie," etc. ...* —Rusty

After their Loch Lomond detour, the girls continued their drive south, eventually reaching the outskirts of Glasgow. Rusty wrote, "The air was so full of soot and smoke we nearly choked, and the entire sky, was gray even though the sun was shining! I don't know <u>how</u> those people can stand it — or can <u>live</u> <u>there</u>!"

After Glasgow, the girls drove through plain, unadorned, grass-covered hills that reminded Rusty of South Dakota.

> *It didn't last long, tho, and then we noticed <u>fields</u> of tall pine trees, surrounded by a neat stone wall; — as if the trees had been planted as you would plant a field of corn!! Stone walls wound over the hills like snakes; and sheep, black faced and black footed, are everywhere. Then we began to notice that <u>all</u> the trees grew and leaned toward the east. The branches looked like they were reaching for something — The wind must blow constantly from that one direction!* —Rusty

Craving a good beef or steak dinner after their long day's drive, the girls looked for a nice cozy inn but couldn't find one. After driving for miles without seeing anything, they saw a brightly lit place up on a hill with "millions" of huge trucks parked all around. Hesitant and with low expectations, the girls went in. According to Kit, the place was grubby, and there were "nothing but truck drivers – all over – munching huge platters of steaming food." The girls ordered steak pie and chips and were surprised at how good it was. "Yummy! Had wonderful peas with it too," Kit wrote in a letter home:

> *Oh, if our families could only see us now!? – Us and 35 truck*
> *drivers munching on steak pie. The radio was playing Brahms and*
> *nobody complained or yelled, "Hey, Mac, cantcha get da ball*
> *game?" Had ice cream and tea also and the whole thing came to*
> *about $0.50 each! Not quite a cozy inn dinner but delicious and*
> *much more interesting atmosphere. Also, nobody made any passes,*
> *wise cracks or even stared at us. —Kit*

In her journal, Kit added a note about the truckers, "Not a flicker from them – so different from American creeps!"

It was about this time that Rusty learned her hometown newspaper, the *Fort Pierre Times*, was now publishing her letters. Rusty wrote her mother in a letter dated October 18, 1954, "It makes me very happy to know he [the editor] is so interested and I enjoy it even more to know that what I see and write about is interesting to others and that you both can enjoy my letters and perhaps share some of all this wondrous world I'm seeing!"

15

Shattering a Window in Northwest England
(October 15 - October 17, 1954)

After a night spent in Penrith, the girls continued their drive south through northwest England. On October 15, Rusty wrote:

> *So far we are very unimpressed with England. Drove through a real pea soup fog this morning for about a half hour — Could only go about 10 miles an hour — a steady stream of cars and we were climbing and then going down a very steep hill. Don't know how the country is so green with all the black smoke! Guess we're in the heart of the industrial section, but every city and town is so terribly gray, — even the <u>people</u> were all gray! — And the towns look gloomy to me. —Rusty*

It happened around dusk. According to Kit, the weather was still horrible, with rain and drizzle all the time. As Kit drove through one of the "innumerable British road construction sections," something thumped Rusty in the chest.

I was going very slowly as you are instructed to do – rounded a curve and suddenly there was a whizz, thump, crack and then a quiet crackle, crackle, crackle. By that time I had pulled over to the side and had my foot on the brake. —Kit

The windshield was completely shattered. Kit wrote, "I tried to look out the windshield to see what had happened but I couldn't – it was a mass of cracks. We were just stunned."

Rusty wrote, "A rock had evidently been spun into the air by one of the ten thousand trucks on the highway today, and it came careening in through our windshield."

According to Kit, there was a hole as big as a lemon right in front of Rusty, "and the window was a hopeless mess. So there we were – out in the country at dusk ... windshield ... sounding like something out of a Kellogg's Rice Krispies box!"

"Thank heavens it was shatter-proof glass, and thank heavens the rock didn't hit one of us in the eye," Rusty wrote. Although Kit wrote her parents that it was she who walked to a nearby farm, Rusty said it was "a man." In either case, a man at the farm phoned a nearby garage. Kit stayed and entertained the family at the farm with her account of the accident and tales of their travels until a "nice young man" from the garage appeared.

He came and knocked out the windshield, and we had to drive back to [Stone] (1 mile) and leave Europa at the garage. Now we're worried about getting a new windshield – it's a French car! Oh my – Also the garage man doesn't think insurance covers this! – I thought I was insured against everything! It's not fair! How much does a new windshield cost? I haven't the vaguest idea. – We'll find out soon enough I guess. —Rusty

After spending the night in Stone, a small town north of Stafford, Kit wrote, "The next morning the garage called to say we were to drive over to the large town (about 7 miles away) as soon as possible, where they could cut a new windshield for us (it being a French car they didn't have one to fit)."

Rusty continued:

We had to take a huge funny English taxi out to our garage – It was kind of like an old touring car — black and of course the driver sat on the right. Seemed so funny – didn't seem like we had a driver! <u>Then</u> we had to drive Europa to Stafford, 5 miles away! – Wish I were a good cartoon artist – she must have made a very funny picture! — The windshield all net, with tiny bits of glass around the edge, clattering to the floor at every bump; it began raining slightly; both had kerchiefs on, and Kit was peering underneath the sun visor, trying to keep the rain and wind out of her eyes. I was wearing sun glasses, and trying to peer between the raindrops was cross-eyed work! If people turned and stared before, you should have seen them today! — Left Europa at the glass place (they had to <u>cut</u> a new windshield for her), and we wandered around Stafford; — fairly good size town; — Meandered wide-eyed through their market. – It's inside, — <u>huge</u>, — and they sell <u>everything</u>!! Stands and booths selling fish, vegetables, shoes, hardware, fruits, toys, meat, all kinds of clothes, candy and cookies, dishes, — Well, it was <u>almost</u> another Maxwell Street! – Bought some apples and then returned to the garage about 2:00 PM – It cost L4/16 (4 pounds, 16 shillings) or around $13.00 – And – we were off again. —Rusty

From Stafford, the girls drove to Warwick. After tea at the Porridge Pot, they continued on to Stratford-Upon-Avon, arriving at dusk with only enough time for a tour of Shakespeare's birth place. Kit and Rusty toured the "wonderful" 400-year old house, including the bedroom where Shakespeare was born, the kitchen and living room. Although they found the names of several famous people etched in the glass window, including Sir Walter Scott, Ellen Terry, and Thomas Carlyle, the girls only signed the guest book.

> *The same stone floor in the living room that was there 4 (four) hundred years ago!!! They have taken good care of it for the last 2 hundred years; — but parts of it are standing exactly – have scarcely been touched! — As they were then. The floors are uphill and down dale – the ceilings look almost ready to fall in. – and yet it's very cozy and soooo interesting!! As I stand in the bedroom where William was born, I had again this strange feeling, — of the centuries vanishing and suddenly everything is timeless – and I'm almost in a dream world. Tried to imagine what the life in that household was like then — and it was too much for me. ... When you come this is one place we must come! I know you'll love it, too!*
> —Rusty

After the tour, the girls discovered that Anne Hathaway's cottage wouldn't be open until 2 p.m. the next day. "Since all the hotels were very touristy and hence very expensive, and adding many things together, decided we'd better not stay all nite. Terribly disappointed, tho; — so we're going to try and go up for a day while we're situated in London," Rusty wrote. The girls left Stratford and searched for an inexpensive place to stay in Oxford.

Finally got a room at a boarding house type place for 12 and 6
(about $1.80) ... So far Great Britain has been the most expensive
country we've been in, — and all the hotels have been <u>much</u> more
than we have been paying! As high as $2.50 each – and that's <u>awful</u>,
when we're used to 1.00 and 1.55 – (Including <u>breakfast</u>!) —Rusty

After breakfast in Oxford, the girls toured the town by foot.

It was just at 10:00 AM and Sunday, and every Church in the
entire city began ringing its bells! – It was perfect! – All these
chimes and bells coming from all corners of this old old city! The
town, and the University are completely intermingled – Doesn't
seem like there's any part of the town without a bldg. or part of the
university, and not part of the school without part of the town right
next to it. – They are one – and so old! It was a beautiful fall day. –
Cloudy but warm, and every once in awhile the sun peeked out for a
couple of seconds (long enough for me to get 2 pictures.) We strolled
around eyeing all the Oxfordian men (ha!) and feeling the calm and
peaceful Sunday atmosphere seep in. – and being a little awed at
this ancient seat of learning- The university was founded in 1240 –
over 700 years ago! Can you imagine? I can't. – Didn't have too
much time to spend there, tho as we wanted to get into London on
Sunday, when the traffic would be at its lowest ebb. Anyway, Chris
Willy (Queen Mary, remember?) promised us a complete and extra
thorough tour of Oxford – so –.   —Rusty

16

Rubbernecking in London
(October 17 – October 20, 1954)

With a promise to return to Oxford with Chris Willy, their friend from the *Queen Mary*, the girls drove "blithely on into London."

"Can you imagine me driving into London???!!!" Rusty wrote to her mother. "On the left side of the street no less?! I DID IT!!! … soon we were passing Hyde Park and Piccadilly Circus and other names that seemed to be suddenly out of fairy books! English bobbies were in the streets helping to direct traffic – and here we were!"

"London is lovely," Kit wrote. "No tremendously tall buildings like New York – had expected grayness and big buildings so we were really excited when we saw how spacious it was."

With the tourist office closed and no reservations, the girls finally parked on a side street, and Kit looked up YWCAs. They found a room at the Bedford House YWCA for four nights. Kit described the Bedford House in her journal:

> *Fabulous! Big room – bath and john right next to us. Several catches (like "lights out" at 11:00!) but we hope we can stay here whole time. No tipping etc. Most inexpensive place in town, I'm sure! Sitting here like 2 naughty school girls now with lights on after 11:00. Lots to see – can't wait til tomorrow.* —Kit

Rusty described Bedford House in a letter:

> *We chose one blindly and called – LADY LUCK is still with us! – Our room is wonderfully big!! (CHEAP) – 10/6 (10 shillings and six pense; — you say ("ten and six") for "bed and breakfast" – cheapest we've ever heard of in Great Britain!!! And of course it's a Y, so we can have other meals here (very inexpensive) and we have a laundry room and an iron to use! And free bathtubs!! And many other little luxuries! Only – terribly funny thing! – Lights out at 11:00! Can you imagine! – There are working women who live there – all over 21 – and they have to put out their lights at 11:00! I'm still getting over the shock- It's now 12:50 – every time we hear footsteps we switch our lights out for a couple minutes – then back on they go. – And – everyone has to be in by 10:30 – and those who live here can only have 2 late nights a week (we have to let them know in the morning if we plan to be out later that night) – I think that's monstrous!! I just don't understand! This is worse than Northwestern Univ. – school, when I agree regulations are helpful but here! – First I get outraged then giggly when we turn these blasted lights off!* —Rusty

After getting settled at the YWCA, the girls walked all around Piccadilly Circus and Leicester Square singing "… goodbye my

Piccadilly, — so long, Leicester Square! It's a long, long way to Tipperary."

With mail their only connection to home and their families, the girls met each new city with anticipation and most often stopped first at the American Express office. Rusty and Kit wrote family and friends their approximate itinerary with the address of the nearest American Express office. Mail was held, at no charge, for up to 30 days and forwarded upon request. From London, Kit wrote, "It killed us when we arrived on Sunday to know [the mail] was all waiting for us here and we couldn't get to it. Dashed down first thing this morning and had to wait 10 minutes – nearly beside ourselves! Your letters were wonderful."

After reading their mail for an hour, Kit and Rusty went back to the theater booking office at American Express. Rusty wrote:

> There stood 2 girls, - I looked at one, couldn't believe my eyes – then slowly carefully said "Sue — ??!!" And it was Sue Goldman!!! Remember the girl I visited in Brooklyn after the summer drama school at Plymouth? ... We were so excited it took us half an hour to calm down. She and another girl have hitch-hiked and bicycled around Europe for four months and are on their way home to USA now. But what a shock! —Rusty

Hopping on the Number 11 bus, Kit and Rusty began to tour London.

> We passed right beside <u>Big</u> <u>Ben</u> – and Westminster Abbey and Buckingham Palace and many other places – Stopped at the end of the line and mosied around an old open-air market in Shepherd's Bush (West section of London). Later had lunch, then went to see

St. Martin-in-the-Fields Church in Trafalgar Square. It is a very old, very charming small Church of England ... historical, too, as everything in London is! —Rusty

Rusty described another "small world" experience at the National Gallery:

We were in the midst of looking at some lovely paintings when this boy, whom I had noticed was staring at me for some time came up to me and asked if I was American, he said he was sure he knew me from somewhere. – I thought "Oh oh, here we go again – This line sounds familiar" – but you should have heard the following conversation – "Ever been to New York?" "Where did you go to school?" etc. – Until finally it came out – He had taken a Columbia course in radio and TV from Warren Jacober, and had remembered me when he had visited **Three Steps to Heaven** *in the studio one day! CAN YOU IMAGINE?? Incredible, really! A* year *ago, — this was – and then in a museum in London- It's* too much*!! You certainly can't "escape" in this world!* Twice *in the same* day*!*
—Rusty

Rusty continued in another letter:

From the museum then, Kit and I called Chris Willy (from the Queen Mary) and John McGovern ... From there we hurried out to Chris' flat (in England an apartment is called a flat) to see him before he kept a dinner engagement. The same Chris – very sweet! — He was so excited to see us! Then we hurried to get to the other end of London to meet John at the end of his class at nite school. He was waiting outside the subway stop, — He's nice looking, short, — and what a talker!! – (ha!) He walked Kit and me for blocks and then we had coffee espresso in a very "arty" little place – He is

much too busy! So the only day we could arrange to meet again
was on Sunday. —Rusty

Chris Willy met the girls the next day right after breakfast and took them to see the Tower of London. The girls were impressed by its size and history. Kit wrote, "Of course, I had always thought that The Tower was just a tower – but it turned out to be an immense castle fortress covering an area of 18 acres! It was built by William the Conqueror and has a long and bloody history."

> *It was built first as a palace, but for <u>centuries</u> it has been a prison and has housed some of the most famous names in history!! ...*

> *A real <u>Beefeater</u> was our guide ... in red and Navy costume. ... He was wonderful! So proud, so dignified and yet so jolly! We learned some fascinating <u>incredible</u> things about the Tower and it brought back so much history that I've read or studied, to me! I bought a book that tells all about it, so I can lend it to you – <u>and</u> remember. ... We stood in the Bloody Tower, where Sir Walter Raleigh spent 13 years of his life before being beheaded ... and in the Bell Tower where Princess Elizabeth (Good Queen Bess) was imprisoned – remember how she <u>hated</u> the Tower? And from that particular tower to the Beauchamp Tower there is a high wall along which Elizabeth could get "fresh air," – this became known as "Elizabeth walk."*
> —Rusty

They were fascinated by stories of beheading and execution. Kit wrote, "Many people were beheaded there – including Queen

Anne Boleyn, the Duke of Buckingham, Queen Katharine Howard and dozens of others."

Our beefeater told us literally hundreds of names of the beheaded persons who were buried here and how unceremoniously they were brought from the block to be interred in the main body of the Chapel. — Far more than they ever really had room for, — the Chapel is really quite small. — And then in another tower the stone walls had names and intricate designs and prayers and moral quotes carved into them. — To picture the men and women who spent years carving these, while they were locked in these cold, gray stone, lightless towers. —-!

Kit, a Beefeater and I in the Tower of London. —Rusty

*Near the Tower was the Tower Bridge which was very picturesque
and very exciting! – Will be able to describe things so much better
when I can show you my pictures, too!! — Near there is a large
green and here was the scene of all the executions of the <u>common</u>
people – Only royalty and important personages had the "honor" to
be beheaded within the Tower walls. —Rusty*

They were mesmerized by the crown jewels. Rusty wrote, "In
the Wakefield Tower many other famous people spent their last
few days, and now it contains the Crown Jewels, 'The dazzling
brilliance as you walk in almost blinds you.'"

Kit wrote:

*They are kept there (and always have been) because it's the strongest
fortress in the land. And they are simply unbelievable! Gorgeous
crowns from kings and queens from way back – studded with
hundreds of precious gems, beautiful coronation rings, maces, etc. –
quite a display! —Kit*

Rusty went into more detail:

*The one [crown] Queen Elizabeth [the Second] wears on state
occasions is <u>beautiful</u>. This type with the purple velvet inside and
solid diamonds, the Star of Africa (one of the two) was set in it; –
looked about the size of a large apricot. – Also saw Queen Victoria's
crown which is <u>tiny</u>! — looks like a baby's! – And the Kohinoor
diamond is set in the Queen Mother's crown! — Beside all the
crowns are the Coronation jewelry, the Coronation dining silver (or
gold) and countless <u>salt</u> <u>cellars</u> – in various shapes and extreme
sizes, — all gold and encrusted with many jewels. The traditional
garter and all its attachments were there for when a knight is made
a member of the Order of the Garter. —Rusty*

"After lapping up the Tower," as Kit wrote, Chris, Kit and Rusty stood on the bank of the River Thames and gazed at the London Bridge. Rusty found the bridge "kind of disappointing because it's been re-modernized and is a plain ordinary bridge."

Chris Willy and Kit at Trafalgar Square.

From the bridge, Chris took the girls for a walk down into the city's business district where the girls were impressed with the buildings as well as the men. Kit described the Bank of England, often called "the Old Lady of Threadneedle Street."

We walking along Threadneedle Street and saw "The Old Lady" – and what an impressive sight that is – immense and solid as the Rock of Gibraltar – now I know where the expression "as safe as the Bank of England" came from! The Mayor's mansion is there too, and just as we were passing by the door opened and out came the Lord Mayor himself in full regalia - all gilt, cocked hat, etc., with a bewigged and bedecorated barrister and a flunkey in livery. We were so excited we were practically jumping up and down!

Must insert a note here about the business men in London. They are wonderful – and unbelievable! They dress in black suits, black bowlers, vests, heavy watch chains and very tightly furled umbrellas and yellow chamois gloves. In "The City" most of them wear striped trousers also. About 60% of the men wear mustaches and/or Van Dyke beards. The mustaches vary considerably from small clipped to long bushy. There is no doubt about the fact that London men are the best dressed in the world. We fell for everyone we passed in the street. Did you know they always carry an umbrella – tightly rolled. Chris told us that usually even if it rains the Londoners don't undo their umbrellas – they would rather walk in the rain then take the 20 minutes required to furl it neatly and tightly enough after the rain is over. —Kit

They walked on to St. Paul's Cathedral, arriving just in time for the afternoon service. The three sat for a while and listened to the boys' choir from St. Paul's School, which Kit described as lovely and a wonderful experience. Surprised at the building's style, Kit wrote, "It is done in classic, not Gothic, style and so looked relatively un-churchy (especially Church of England) to me. Inside it is lovely – it is immense (second largest in the world – St. Peter's in Rome is first) but yet gives a feeling of warmth."

17

Sipping Sherry in Oxford and Tea in London
(October 21 – October 26, 1954)

Upholding his promise of a personal tour of Oxford, Chris Willy met the girls on Thursday, October 21, and drove "about 2 hours through lovely green rolling English countryside" from London to Oxford. Rusty wrote, "It was a lovely sunshiny day, — we drove through pretty wooded hills, with our roof open!! – Stopped at a <u>very</u> <u>old</u> English pub at the side of the road (it was built in the <u>1500s</u>!!! <u>Adorable</u>!) and had sandwiches and I had <u>tea</u> while Chris and Kit had beer."

Following are descriptions of the day written by both Kit and Rusty.

> *Oxford is simply beautiful. I could spend weeks there just wandering around and looking. The town itself is charming – lovely little old houses, winding streets – and, of course, the main part of it*

is made up by the beautiful ancient colleges. They date from the 12th, 13th, 14th, etc. centuries. Each one is different from the other and yet they all harmonize beautifully. —Kit

In Oxford, we walked all about the various colleges – so <u>terribly old</u>. – and the buildings all have so much <u>character</u>! One of the colleges is called "New College," – it was built in the 13th century! – <u>Seven hundred years ago</u>! And boys are living in and studying in the SAME ROOMS that men did <u>then</u>!!! It's absolutely incredible and so <u>completely</u> fascinating!) No one can ever see Oxford really unless they're shown it by an Oxford student. ... We were so lucky to have Chris with us – he graduated from Lincoln College at Oxford and so was able to take us into the most interesting colleges and show us around – something we wouldn't have been able to do on our own. —Rusty

We went into [Merton College Library] *the oldest existing library [for university scholars and students] in the world! ... Chris found a janitor-type-person to unlock the door and he was so <u>proud</u> of it, he sort of "took over" from Chris and beaming showed us all around. – Dark dark wood! Very old-English style – medieval – Huge volumes upon volumes of <u>hand</u>-written "knowledge" were <u>chained</u> in the bookcases; and narrow hard wooden benches ran parallel to each bookcase – these were for the students; — they had to sit there while they studied from the books which were chained. And the only light <u>then</u> came from slit-like windows: how anyone kept from going blind I'll never know!* —Rusty

They still have quite a few of the original books there – we saw several volumes on early herbal medicine which are still chained to the shelves the way they were in the old days so that no one would steal them. They also had there the original old wooden chest in

which the first books were kept. It has three enormous locks on it and the three keys were kept by 3 different men so no one of them could open the chest alone. Thus did they keep a close check on one another — how precious their books were then — and look how we throw them around today! —Kit

Chris showed us everything, including the dining room in <u>his</u> college (named <u>Lincoln</u> College); — it was the type you might imagine King Arthur ate in! — The dark rich wood, fireplace, OLD OLD OLD, — candles, — too hard to describe; but what an atmosphere to dine in! It is all so <u>terribly</u> full of tradition and <u>scholarly</u> atmosphere. — not rah rah Joe College like most of our universities, — but more the university of great and noble minds — Really, the contrast is fascinating! Oxford is a little world all its own. —Rusty

As Chris took the girls around Oxford, they passed several beautiful chapels from the 13th and 14th centuries and "wandered along the river where the boys take their girls punting and where the sculling teams practice." Kit wrote about seeing undergraduates running around in "little short black gowns" while their professors wore full-length gowns. Everybody rode bicycles "from the deans on down."

After tea at a "lovely old 15th century hotel in town where the London stage used to stop," the three entered Worcester College at dusk to have sherry in another student's room.

Walked through [a] beautiful garden courtyard and into a crumbling stone tunnel like archway; — knocked at old wooden door; — and David Tankard invited us into his "suite;" — (they <u>all</u> have 2 or 3 rooms) a fire was going in the fireplace, and another English boy, David Galloway, was there, too. They had sherry while

I had a kind of orange pop (which they call orange squash in England) – not very good, I must say. – But Kit and I were highly amused and entertained by the 3 very British young Oxford students! What an odd race Great Britain breeds! More individualistic, I think, than any other group of people! —Rusty

Rusty didn't drink before her trip to Europe, but by the time she came home, she appreciated a glass of wine now and then. Although she wrote her mother that she was only drinking orange pop in Oxford, she later remembered being convinced to try a taste of cognac or sherry while sitting by the fire.

"People dropped in and out while we were there and it was all very charming," Kit wrote.

"All five of us then drove to Woodstock to the coziest most adorable little inn for dinner!" Rusty wrote.

"You should have seen us fitting into tiny little Europa – but we managed," Kit told her family. According to Kit, the meal was the "best dinner we had in England."

A man and his wife run the whole thing and they were so sweet and quaint and friendly! I'd say that except for their fabulous teas, the English food is the most un-interesting of any – including certainly the United States – They boil everything – and boil out the flavor – But this meal was quite delicious! —Rusty

After dinner, the five (according to Rusty) or six (according to Kit), squeezed back into the car and drove to one of the favorite spots of Oxford social life, the Trout. Rusty described it as "a special 'hidden away' hangout of the Oxford men and their dates." She wrote, "It was another 16th Century inn, built right on the banks of the Thames River, — with a small waterfall roaring beside the patio; — a fireplace in every tiny room; — lots of students — Mmm — we loved it!"

On their way back to Oxford, the car engine died. "I kept saying that the gas was getting LOW," Rusty wrote.

> *But no one took me very seriously, I guess, — and we couldn't see a gas station — And <u>just</u> as we got into the center of Oxford, the motor stopped! The first time Europa has ever run out of gas! — And there ensued one of the funniest scenes you've ever seen! Discovered there was only one gas station open in town and that was many blocks away. — Everyone got out to push, while I sat in and steered. — It's such a tiny light little car, that soon they discovered it didn't need much pushing! David Galloway (after it got started) was pushing it with one hand, and the choice remark of the evening was "Why, it's just like pushing a <u>pram</u>!" (Pram is the English word for baby buggy) — David T., Chris and Kit lagged behind, laughing so hard they could hardly walk as David G. called to some fellow students on the sidewalk to come help. — they only hurried when he said there was an American girl inside. — For nearly a block there were 6 Oxford men pushing Europa and me. Then I looked up to find two men on <u>bicycles</u>, one on either side of me, pushing! They each had one hand in the open roof and were pedaling along <u>pushing</u> me. — I was laughing so hard I could hardly see — but made it to the filling station in <u>record</u> time!!*
> —Rusty

After four nights at the Bedford House YWCA, the girls moved into the Eccleston YWCA, which Kit described as the "most horrible place." Because they shared the new room with two other girls, there was no space for all of their luggage. Fed up with

YWCAs, the girls moved the next night to an inexpensive private hotel where all the other occupants were English young men. Kit said later that the young men were "all blue collar kids who were going on to higher education. They wouldn't talk to us. They were shy."

"It was a very basic place," Kit said. "In order to take a hot water bath, you had to make an appointment. You met the lady who ran the bed and breakfast in the hallway outside the door. Then she handed you the knob for the hot water (faucet handle)." She added, "That was a shocker."

After spending most of the day Friday moving, washing clothes, and shopping, the girls met up with David Tankard, and two of his friends, Tim (a businessman) and Stephen (a barrister) who were in town over the weekend. The three of them "squired us around the city on Saturday," according to Kit.

> *They all were in the market for some <u>antiques</u> to help furnish and decorate their rooms or apts; — so we went to an open-air antique market!! A very high class version of <u>part</u> of Maxwell St. in Chicago! – Heard lots of the <u>Cockney</u> accents! And stopped on a street corner and listened to a soap box orator who was a conservative ... very humorous! – The morning and afternoon were really very interesting; — we saw a part of London that the <u>tourist</u> <u>never</u> sees! – The boys wouldn't let Kit and me talk, because they said as soon as our American accents were heard the prices would go bounding way up! —Rusty*

Kit wrote, "It was great to be with the English lads because they acted as sort of a good cover for us – if we'd been alone our Americanism would have stuck out all over and we wouldn't have had a chance to sneak around and eavesdrop inconspicuously."

After seeing David off on the 4:00 train to Kent, Stephen, Tim, Kit, and Rusty went to Tim's apartment for tea. "The Englishman, come Hell or High water, will <u>never</u> miss his tea!!!" Rusty wrote.

Chris said that even the <u>Army</u> will stop by the side of the road, on command of the head officer, — and out will come small cooking stoves and pans of water – and tea — Over tea and biscuits (cookies to us) the 4 of us talked with much animation about the contrasts between American and English dating habits, social pressure, clothing, language, — even F.D. Roosevelt – Many laughs and a very good time! —Rusty

Rusty and Kit with John McGovern at Windsor.

"And the next day was Sunday the 24th — and Kit and I picked John McGovern and Josie, his girl, up, and then drove to Windsor," Rusty continued:

John noticed the Queen's Standard was flying; — and sure enough when we asked a Bobbie about seeing inside the Castle, he said No; — and that the Queen was dining in the left wing right then! — — So we decided we should dine, too. – Had fish and chips – (Chips are French-fried potatoes and crisps are what we call potato chips).

Really it's quite indescribable, it's so big. None of the interior was open for inspection except the beautiful St. George Chapel. This was worth the whole trip. It is a magnificent piece of architecture – of the "perpendicular" school of late medieval times. It gives a tremendous impression of light, space and airiness because of its straight up and down lines and because of the slimness of the inside columns which support it – yet it is a warm and comfortable place without any of the other cold echoyness found in so many large stone churches. Henry VIII and his third wife are buried there in a vault in the middle of the Choir loft and there are five other kings and queens buried in chapels, etc., around the church. What a strange feeling it is to walk down the aisle and suddenly find yourself standing right on Henry the VIII's grave! —Rusty

While they were exploring St. George Chapel, the girls encountered their first Eton boy:

Rusty and I were wandering around gazing wide-eyed as usual when we were suddenly spoken to in the hushed and pearl like tones of Eton – turned around there was a young (about 16) Eton lad in full regalia … who wanted to know if we would like to be shown around the church – we gulped and said "sure." So he did – delightfully too! This is evidently a service which Eton (right nearby) performs for tourists and each boy has his turn at it. We were there on a Sunday and the place was mobbed with Eton boys – from grammar school on up. —Kit

The little Eton boys are adorable! All ages from about 8 up to 17 we saw there – and all wearing their striped trousers, black tails, bow ties, and gloves and carrying black furled umbrellas. I didn't know they really <u>wore</u> these clothes, but it's <u>standard</u> dress for them all the time! I was clever and got a very good picture of 2 of them, I think — We drove through Eton on our way back to London. – John and Josie had plans that nite, so after dropping them off, Kit and I decided to go to a real English movie. ... Goodness! I've been writing for nearly 2 hours – I'm exhausted – to bed. —Rusty

Back in London on Monday, October 25, the girls were excited to see the sun. Rusty wrote, "We awoke and saw blue sky and SUN, so with screams of joy we grabbed our cameras and went tearing outside – Drove Europa because we were afraid if we didn't <u>hurry</u>, the sun would slip behind a bit of fog."

They spent the day sightseeing. Rusty wrote:

Took pictures in Trafalgar Square, then drove to Whitehall where the Changing of the <u>Horse Guard</u> takes place – Terribly impressive!!! About 20 men on horse back came riding all the way from Buckingham Palace to relieve 20 others – It all took place in a large courtyard ... and it was so dignified and to think they've been doing this for centuries! It's very hard to describe, — but the men who were relieved were dressed in high black shiny boots, <u>blue</u> capes spread out over the saddle and all about them, swords, shiny silver helmets with long red silken tassels. – in the sunlight they were brilliant! And the others who were coming on "duty" were dressed the same except that they wore red capes and <u>blue</u> tassels – All the *horses were coal shiny black; — only a very few had a white foot or a white star. Even their <u>hooves</u> were polished black – And they were so well trained – beautiful!!! We stood near an archway opening into the courtyard, and from an opposite archway exactly at 11:00 AM came the red caped guards, led by a man in a more elegant different shade-of-red cape, on a white horse, and blowing a bugle. Then the reds lined up on one side and the blues on the other, — the leader from each group met in the center and talked for a long time, — And then the reds took their places and the blues rode out — The dignity and the seriousness with which the English sustain all these ritualistic customs is really amazing; — Must admit I kind of liked it! It was very heart-stirring; — and really thrilling!* —Rusty*

Kit added:

The changing takes about a half hour and is done very slowly with great ceremony … each regiment has a trumpeter who dresses in an even fancier uniform. He blows all the commands on his gold trumpet with the regiment standard hanging from it. It is so thrilling to hear the sharp notes of the trumpet and to watch the two lines of troops facing each other slowly draw their swords and salute each other. Really, we just love all the pomp and circumstance in England. —Kit

"Went to Westminster Abbey next," Kit wrote. "(Doesn't that sound fantastic – still can't believe we're seeing all these things we've heard so much about!)"

The girls took photos of Big Ben, the Houses of Parliament and the exterior of Westminster Abbey before spending several hours wandering inside Westminster. Rusty wrote, "It's a very large cathedral with statues upon statues and vaults upon vaults and name placques on every available inch of space – the statues are of England's noble men and women."

The girls looked at the inscriptions, stood in the center and imagined the Coronation, and were surprised when they suddenly discovered they were standing on some famous person's grave. Rusty wrote, "The most exciting moment was when we discovered the 'Poet's Corner;' we looked down, and there at our very feet were the tombs (in the floor) of Robert Browning and Shelley!!!"

Kit wrote:

> *We were standing on Browning's grave, right next to him was Tennyson – turned around and there was Chaucer. Of course, by this time we were completely ga-ga with excitement – didn't dare scream but stood there squeaking and clutching each other saying, "Look, look!"* —Kit

"Then we stood by the tombs and epitaphs of Tennyson, Keats, Dickens, Jonson, Kipling, Goldsmith, Chaucer, Hardy, — George Frederic Handel! – and many many others! It was overwhelming!" Rusty wrote.

According to Kit, "One of the most thrilling to me was G.F. Handel. There was also a plaque on the wall near his grave telling of the memorial service held in Westminster for him – playing his music – and who conducted and all the royalty which were present."

"The tomb of the unknown soldier is very simple and very impressive," Kit wrote, while Rusty embellished "[…] And tears rose again when I stood by the grave of England's unknown soldier – 'He is laid among Kings.'"

Kit added:

> *Anyway – Westminster was fascinating – oh – almost forgot, they also have in a chapel in Westminster the old coronation chair in which every monarch has been crowned since 1200 something, containing the famous Stone of Scone. The chair is really terribly worn – and very plain – not too well designed – the gilt is almost all worn off the back but what a feel to look at it and think of all the royal personages who have occupied it through the centuries; struggles they have gone through just to gain the honor of sitting in it – and what their struggles eventually brought them.* —Kit

After tea, the girls accompanied Chris to his flat for cocktails. According to Rusty, they just talked and relaxed while Chris showed them color slides of his trip to the USA.

> *Then he took us to a little Italian restaurant in Chelsea (the "equal" of Greenwich Village), where, Chris said, Princess Margaret Rose comes often! – And that night we had a real London fog!! — The only one we saw in London – we loved it! — - Oh yes, and I nearly forgot: that day we saw DOWNING STREET; — and accidentally we parked right by SCOTLAND YARD!!* —Rusty

On October 26, another sunny, but hazy, day in London, Kit and Rusty joined Sue Goldman (Rusty's friend from Brooklyn) and Chris Willy in front of Buckingham Palace to watch the changing of the guards.

"They look just like toy soldiers! And they are so perfect! Splendid marching!" Rusty wrote of the changing of the guards. Because her standard was flying, the girls knew Queen Elizabeth II was "at home," again.

Just as we were leaving we noticed 2 red and gold carriages by a palace door inside the Courtyard. – As if it were a hundred years ago – Then, a little man dressed in black came out of the Palace, climbed into the carriage, assisted by two men in long bright red cloaks who then climbed up to their positions at the back of the carriage; — the driver cracked his whip and off they went. No one seemed to know who the "important person" was, but it was exciting anyway! —Rusty

After Buckingham Palace, the girls decided to do a little shopping on Bond Street.

But, though the shops were very elegant, we couldn't find anything we liked; — so went to the Burlington Arch which is actually a more exclusive and lovely shopping district for men. Bought a very English-looking tie for Rex [friend of her mother] *– wish it could be something more exciting but don't think he'll wear a vest or a cravat or carry an umbrella – all of which are so typically English and really are lovely in London.* —Rusty

Rusty called the British Museum "fabulous," and Kit called it "marvelous." Kit was thrilled with its exhibits, especially the section of manuscripts and documents.

Saw the Magna Carta, ancient Bibles, Rosetta Stone and dozens of original manuscripts and musical scores. They have an original of [Thomas] *Gray's Elegy, Rob't. Burns' diary (read a page of it) and hundreds of original manuscripts by all the people I mentioned who were buried at Westminster plus many, many others – it is wonderful to look at the different handwritings and various personal messages of some of the most famous writers and composers in the world.* —Kit

Rusty wrote:

> *What a mood this puts me in! – Also there were sheets of the*
> *original music by Mozart, Beethoven, Bach, Chopin, Handel,*
> *Wagner – all of them!! WONDERFUL!! And all with their changes*
> *and little notes and reminders they had scribbled on the margins –*
> *Absolutely TORE ourselves away (I could spend a week just*
> *pouring over each and every word all of them had written!) – But*
> *we had to change into fancy dress … and meet Chris. —Rusty*

"That night we went to the 'Old Vic' and saw a blood and thunder performance of Macbeth," Kit wrote. "Really quite overpowering. Enjoyed it very much. Love English theaters – they serve tea at your seat during intermission."

According to Rusty, "To actually be at the Old Vic Theatre was almost as exciting as the play. Macbeth was done in the old style, — a little too much 'gore' and shouting for me, but it was very entertaining anyway!"

18

Taking in the Theater
in Stratford-Upon-Avon
(October 27, 1954)

"Oct. 27th was a glorious, glorious day!" wrote Rusty, the day she, Kit, and Chris spent in Stratford-Upon-Avon.

> *It is my very favorite town of all so far (excepting PARIS) – a beautiful little 16th Century English village on the banks of the lovely peaceful River Avon. – Since we had been to Shakespeare's birthplace last time, we just went to Anne Hathaway's cottage … and imagined young William walking from his house several minutes away to court Anne; — leaned out of the window in her room and pictured William down below – The low ceilings, tiny, chopped up rooms, narrow stairs; bed with woven thatched mattresses; — fireplaces with kettles hanging in them; — the oven that Anne's mother actually baked in, — charred to show [how] much use was made of it, — Stone slab floors, — YOU MUST see it!!!*

Rusty's drawing of Anne looking out at William.

From there we hurried through the sunny streets to the new Shakespeare Memorial Theatre, and saw the most brilliant magnificent production of THE TAMING OF THE SHREW, — Never have I seen Shakespeare done so beautifully! PERFECTION!! And after the curtain had gone down I reluctantly arose, — and then we had tea in the Theatre's glassed-in-veranda overlooking the Avon River – it was just twilight, — swans were floating in the water, — THE WORLD WAS ALL A ROSY MIST to me – I was off in a warm little dream world – Would love to live in Stratford for a summer! —Rusty

Kit wrote, "Really, it was as though a spell had been cast over us – this will certainly be one of my most treasured memories."

The two drove with Chris to a little town near Oxford and another of his favorite spots. While Kit wrote, "Had a wonderful dinner and toasted our parting of the ways with much wine, etc." Rusty wrote her mother that they had demitasse in the lounge. Whatever they drank, according to Rusty, it was "sort of a farewell to Chris and England."

Rusty wrote on a postcard to her mother on October 27, "Know you'll forgive me for not writing – have had a real 'whirl' in London and it's been wonderful!"

> We left London very sadly the next afternoon. It was another warm, sunny day, and we drove out with the top pushed back – saying goodbye to all the familiar places as we drove by. We really loved London – want to go back some day and see the hundreds of things we missed. —Rusty

19

Crossing the English Channel
(October 28 - October 29, 1954)

From London, the girls drove about an hour and a half southeast to Canterbury, where they stopped for a quick tour late Thursday afternoon. Kit wrote, "We stood in the courtyard as dusk was falling and listened to the bells pealing in the church tower. Then had our last English tea and drove on to Dover."

Dead tired when they arrived in Dover, Rusty and Kit stopped at the first hotel near the docks, the White Cliffs Inn.

> It looked modest so I went in, — when [the woman at the desk] said the room was 24 shillings each ($3.46) I said rather sadly, "Do you have anything for a little less?" She pondered and then quoted a pound each (20 shillings or $2.80); — I looked crestfallen, shook my head dejectedly, — and she said, "I know how it is, — I'll let you have the room for 15 shillings!" – ($2.10) I nearly kissed her! If I

Kit at the White Cliffs of Dover.

ever go to Dover again I shall stay there and willingly pay a huge price! – And our room was delightful! —Rusty

That night, October 28, Rusty wrote a short but overdue letter to her mother.

Dearest Mom,

I'm exhausted – What a whirlwind London was. – I simply can't write much tonite – Must get some sleep for a change!

This is a lovely hotel! Our room is overlooking the channel (near the docks — and you can hear the waves!!!) — Tomorrow we sail at 10:00 AM –from Dover to Boulogne, France — Felt sad as we drove out of London, — I became very attached to her!!

I bought this paper and now I don't have time to write a nice letter on it but I must quickly mail it because I'll soon be out of the country and it will be no good. –

Next morn:

Fell asleep there. Now I've had 10 hours of blissful rest and feel wonderful but have to dash to get on the ferry boat – It's cloudy and I fear the channel may be rough – Wind is blowing too –

Will write soon, I promise!!! Will be in Paris tonite, I hope –

Hello to all.

Much love,

Marialyce

The girls drove to the ferry in howling wind and driving rain, with the radio reporting gale winds on the English Channel. Excited to actually see the famous white cliffs of Dover, Kit and Rusty boarded the ferry at 10:15 in a mist and stood on deck "while it got rougher and rougher."

*And there looming up above us were the WHITE CLIFFS – As white and grand as I had always imagined. – The wind blew and howled, the waves were high and white capped! – We stood on the stern deck as the ferry pulled away from shore, and met with sea spray. We were completely entranced. – Sea gulls flew in large droves about us, and the white cliffs, majestically ethereal, faded into the distance. –*Rusty

When it began to rain, the girls dashed inside and sat in the lounge. When Rusty began to feel funny, a steward came over and said he thought they'd do better on deck. Kit wrote:

He hustled us into our coats and helped us up the stairs - guess I must have been turning green without realizing it – just made it up on deck and in a flash of a second I felt the most peculiar I have ever felt in my life! Hadn't the slightest inkling I was going to be sick – it all happened so quickly. ... Everybody was standing around with these little enamel buckets in hand, and I was no exception. —Kit

View of the White Cliffs of Dover from the ferry.

Kit sat out on deck on a soaking wet bench in the "driving rain and screaming wind feeling awful," while Rusty escaped to the stern.

[I] stood in rain and wind, clutching the railing to keep from being hurled overboard, and tried to think of other things. ... Kept my jaws clenched tightly together – and talked to myself – MADE IT! – The Channel crossing only took an hour and a half, but it was much worse than the North Sea. —Rusty

"Mom, you'd be finished for good after 5 minutes I'm afraid – you'd better stick to the Hoboken ferry!" wrote Kit. "Took us many hours to recuperate. Spent most of these driving down a wet France on our way to Paris."

In Kit's letter home, her first in almost two weeks, she wrote:

Dear Mom and Pops –

Well, aren't I the prize bum! Haven't written since the 19th. I feel terrible! Don't know where the time went – but it was all wonderful! Fell madly in love for the 10 days we were there in London – but don't worry – I'm in Paris now and all is forgotten.
—Kit

BRITISH
ISLES

English Channel

THE NETHERLANDS

Dover

Boulogne

BELGIUM

GERMANY

LUXEMBOURG

Luxembourg

Reims

Paris

Provins

Fontainebleau

Chaumont

FRANCE

SWITZERLAND

Paris and Luxembourg

Well, it had to happen – as it does to all uninsured 26-year old, blondish, female, blue-eyed American tourists in Luxembourg, Europe, during the month of November – yup – I was robbed!

~Kit Tucker

20

Returning to Paris
(October 29 – November 2, 1954)

"It was dusk as we entered the outskirts of Paris, – We were both feeling very gay," Rusty wrote after successfully driving into Paris.

It may be much smaller than London. And it may be on the right side of the road instead of the crazy English left; but – at least in London everyone pays some attention to rules, — in Paris they just go willy-nilly – Your head needs to be on a pivot – cars seem to be coming at you from every direction constantly! It's wild! – We didn't have a hotel, and our previous one was too expensive we have decided, so we picked from our Michelin Guide book one of the cheapest hotels, and wound through chopped up, twisting one-way streets and finally found it – the Grandes Hotel de Lion d'Argent (the Silver Lion) and had a very nice room for 725 francs (about $1.50 each); felt terribly lucky. —Rusty

After a "marvelous dinner" of potage ("that wonderful soup that only <u>France</u> can make!" according to Rusty), sole, green beans and potatoes, and grapes for dessert, Kit wrote, "Boy, it was good to get back to French cooking! Rusty even had a glass of wine with her dinner and said it tasted wonderful!"

Rusty and Kit spent the next morning exploring one of the largest and most visited art museums in the world, Musée du Louvre. Rusty described the Louvre as "a stupendous thing." She wrote:

> *And in the Louvre we saw, gracefully standing in the center of a large domed round room – the VENUS DE MILO – the real one!!! Stood and gazed for many long minutes. — And then as we walked into a large spacious grand hallway bordered by tall marble columns — far down at the end rose a wide marble staircase and far at the top was the Winged Victory; — peaceful and majestic, and appearing to be poised ready for flight at that very second. – Catching our breath we halted and stared in awe. – Later, at a closer view, we inspected her more closely – <u>Beautiful</u>!!! And my favorite of all. — We'll send you a postcard of her, but it's nothing to the way she looks when you're right there! — Then we walked blocks through ancient Greek and Roman statues and findings, through tapestried rooms, heavy ornate furniture and rich Italian paintings hung on enormous walls, — - till we came to a very unassuming small portrait: — Mona Lisa — To actually be seeing these things, — the originals – Wonderful. —Rusty*

Museum weary, the girls left the Louvre and went from "the sublime to the ridiculous." After eating dinner and dressing up back at the hotel, the girls headed to Folies-Bergère, a Parisian music hall made famous by Edouard Manet's 1882 painting, "A

Bar at the Folies-Bergère." Rusty described the theater as lush and dramatic, and Kit wrote:

> It really is quite amazing – the production is fantastic – in fact it is all – the songs and routines are only mediocre. Their staging is so elaborate that they will have 30-40 people on stage for maybe 3 minutes or less in a scene which takes about a minute and the costumes will be plushy and gorgeous and the set too – and you never see them again throughout the entire rest of the performance. It must cost them trillions of dollars! At intermission time you promenade around the gorgeous lobby dripping with gilt and crystal chandeliers and stop for a drink at one of the two huge bars or buy a painting at the art gallery or souvenirs at the souvenir counter.
> —Kit

Rusty described a few of the acts in more detail:

> One set was of a gigantic gold bird cage suddenly coming slowly down from the high domed ceiling above the audience; — and a lovely blonde girl dressed in pink feathers was perched on a swing inside, singing. She had a very pretty voice, and the act was actually breath taking and stunning. … As the song was ending, the bird cage was gradually raised to the dome of the theatre again, and the girl disappeared in the ceiling. In some numbers an entire chorus of men and women would be silver – faces, hands, and elaborate 18th century costumes. – [In] One number, two "stage fulls" of people were dressed and made up to look EXACTLY like Dresden China figurines!! I still don't know how they did it – it was fantastic!

> And then there were numbers which involved nude women and nude men (except for only a "fig leaf"); — they danced, — were extremely graceful and almost cat-like, and it can be compared in no way to any one of the "Burlesques" in the United States. … Here

you were hardly aware of it, and the French accept it as any other
number – They are most "adult" about it, if you know what I mean
— They think nothing of it – It's not treated as a risque moment,
and with an eager gleam in the eye. ... Anyway, we did enjoy the
Folies and I think it's definitely a part of Paris that people should
see.   —Rusty

The following day, a Sunday, the girls met a friend of Kit's, Merriman Holst, who used to work at NBC and was in Europe for three or four months, spending most of it in Paris.

It was fun to see Merriman and compare our trips. He was on the
Dutch ship the beginning of October which collided with a freighter
off the New England coast. Said it was quite an experience. He was
in bed when it happened. He said the whole ship sort of leaped up
and then just shuddered – he looked out his porthole and there in
front of him was the prow of another ship. They made it back to New
York, and he came over finally on the Liberte and loved it. —Kit

The three friends drove around the city and took photos of Paris in the sunshine, climbing to the top of the Eiffel Tower. Rusty wrote on a postcard to her mother, "This is wonderful! The most beautiful view imaginable – We're at the very top!! Sunny day! Paris is more exciting than ever – Wish you were here." She wrote more details several days later in a letter dated November 11.

Kit and I went clear up to the very top of the Eiffel Tower. The Seine
River is lovely – like a dark green jewel winding through the
marvelous streets of Paris ... and we could see the Sacre Coeur
(large white Romanesque style Church) which is high on a hill in
the midst of and overlooking Montmarte (the Artists and Bohemian
section) – Lovely! Then we all drove down to Fontainebleau, which

was the summer home for all the Louis's; and later the favorite
residence of Napoleon. It was very large also, and the same type of
palace as Versailles only on a much smaller scale — a bit warmer and

Me — on top of Eiffel Tower — view of Paris. —Rusty

not as fiercely ornate. Saw his bedroom (Napoleon's) and his throne
room. — the throne he sat in and the famous hat he wore. —Rusty

Sipping Pernod, the three sat at a sidewalk café, La Coupole, for
2 hours in the early evening watching the passing parade before
having dinner at a "real French little restaurant down some
winding side street" and ate sausage on thick crisp-crusted bread,
beefsteak, mounds of fresh green beans, bread, wine, Camembert
cheese, and a banana for $1.16 per person. Rusty wrote:

And in slight desperation I asked for "toilette" (pronounced
twalette), AND — through the kitchen into a tiny courtyard filled

with garbage cans, black and white cats, and baby buggies, — I came to a tiny "outhouse." – Inside there was a hole in the floor. – That's all. – Came back giggling. Had heard this was quite frequently the case of the toilette. – But it was the first we had bumped into!

I never did get that letter on bathrooms written, did I? – Well, let me intercept here a moment then, to tell you of the small round

Drawing in a letter home by Rusty of a vespasienne.

"things" on the streets throughout Paris: for men – In the middle of main intersections, fashionable shopping districts – it makes no difference. … There on the sidewalk is one of these. A man walks in, — you see his head, his feet and legs – There is certainly no shame or embarrassment here!! (ha!) Some are more revealing than others – It's very hard to keep eyes averted and a straight face, believe me!
—Rusty

After dinner, the three hopped into Europa and explored the night city.

First we drove to the middle of the Champs Elysées – what a fabulous view! The Champs is about three times as wide as Fifth Avenue – huge trees on either side – the street slopes up toward the Arc at the end – a lovely vista and at night with the lights on either side of the road all the way up and the floodlights on the Arc it is really breathtaking. Our next stop was Notre Dame. This was our first view of it (we missed it last trip), and I am so glad it turned out to be at night. It is a magnificent and awesome sight. We parked the car and walked slowly all around it. It was a beautiful night – clear and warm. The church is on an island right in the middle of the Seine so we walked down along the banks of that most beautiful river and watched the shimmering white reflection of Notre Dame in the water. It is really quite impossible to describe – I wish we could have a picture of it that way. —Kit

We walked down steps then to the very edge of the Seine. Remember in An American in Paris *when Gene Kelly and Leslie Caron danced at nite along the river? And they came down the steps leading to the street, to this wide cobblestone way beside the Seine? – There we were!* —Rusty

From those steps, Kit and Rusty took Merriman to l'Abbaye in the French Quarter. Although Rusty and Kit had visited the one-room bar with Cherie on their first visit to Paris, this is the first time it is described in one of their letters. Rusty wrote:

It's only one <u>very</u> small room; — <u>smaller</u> than our front room at home! And there is a tiny bar, and <u>tiny</u> tables and old wooden chairs; — people can get one drink and sit there <u>all</u> nite - And there are two Americans, (one is Negro) who were soldiers stationed in Paris during the war and liked it so much they came back to <u>live</u>. They each play the guitar and sing folk songs ... the best I have ever heard! I am completely enchanted as soon as I walk in there. They *are SUPERB!!! What they can do with those guitars is unbelievable; — and they almost act out all their songs – They have been there for 5 years now and have had countless offers to go "up" – but they have found what they like and have the courage to turn down more money and fame for this – They're wonderful! Also, at 12:00 they turn out the lights and from then until closing at 1:30, there are only lighted <u>candles</u>. … <u>And</u> the neighboring people complained because of the noise, so no one is allowed to clap – for applause everyone must snap their fingers; — Otherwise they will be evicted. – A <u>delightful</u> place! — Home then at 2:00. —*Rusty

After breakfast of an omelette and grapes, the girls dashed all around sunny Paris to take more photos. It was All Saints' Day or La Touissant, a Catholic holiday honoring all the saints recognized by the Roman Catholic Church. They gazed at Sacre Coeur and then "poked around Montmartre." Rusty wrote:

*The "home" of Van Gogh, Toulouse Lautrec, Gaugin and all the others, - and Oscar Wilde, too – It was <u>perfect</u>! Tiny streets, crumbling and kind of dirty bldgs., the colorful, sidewalk cafés everywhere, and men painting along the sidewalk – Lovely Sacre Coeur in the background, and Paris laid out at her feet – so much character! This was All Saints' Day and a national holiday, so all the Frenchmen were out enjoying the sun – We sat in a little square amid artists and old men in berets and had coffee. —*Rusty

The girls arrived at Notre Dame just in time for a special All Saints Day service.

What a beautiful church it is inside – the stained glass windows are magnificent – we went up to the gallery above the altar where you get a wonderful view of the entire church and stayed there for an hour and a half just watching the sun pour through the rose

windows – making lovely colored patterns on the high vaulted
ceilings and listening to the voices of the boys' choir floating above
us. You could spend days in the cathedral just looking at it! —Kit

Kit and Rusty on the Place de la Concorde

After the service, the girls walked along the banks of the Seine.
Rusty described stalls, set up on the sidewalk with a wide
selection of books, old and new. Paintings, original and otherwise,
were being sold by little old Frenchmen in berets and moustaches.

We wandered, searching idly for a book in English, when someone
took hold of my arm, and I heard "No, - it couldn't be!" – I turned,
and there was <u>Judy Warden</u>! A girl I was in many plays with at
Northwestern! - She was kind of a "character" in Speech School –
and then she came to N.Y. – I bumped into her at NBC one day and
it was thru Evelyn and me that she eventually became a guidette!
And she had an apt only 3 blocks away from us; … And here we

accidentally met on the street near Notre Dame in Paris. –
Impossible! But true! So she, Kit, and I found a sidewalk café, had
hot chocolate and <u>TALKED</u>! She came to Paris from N.Y. about 5
weeks previous, and was living in Montmartre, taking acting
classes (and being arty). – She was busy that nite, tho, - so we made
very tentative plans to meet in Rome around Christmas or New
Year's time. —Rusty

On their last day in Paris, the errands they thought would take
an hour, took several. "We were due to leave Paris on Tuesday
about 12:00 noon," Kit wrote. "But it turned out to be 'one of those
days.'"

Everything went wrong. We were to collect the insurance money for
the new windshield in Paris (per instructions from London).We had
been told it wouldn't take long so at 9:30 we were at the insurance
office – two and one half hours later we were at our third different
place still trying to get our money – after having filled out a
different form at each place and being sent with it on to the next
place at the other end of the city! Finally, the man said oh yes – we
would get our money there only he was so sorry but it was 12:02
and the cashier's office was closed until 2:00 could we come back at
2:30. So – that was the way the day went – we still [hadn't] done
any of the other little things we were supposed to do so finally at
5:30 p.m. we pulled out of Paris. —Kit

Planning to spend the night at a friend of Rusty's in Chaumont,
165 miles away, the girls were behind schedule. Kit wrote, "We
had tried to get her on the phone several times ... but there was
no answer."

Rusty described their efforts, "The French phone system is the most impossible thing you can imagine!! No one uses it as a convenience or as a useful instrument, but rather they attack it as if it were their enemy!"

> *What was worse was that Kit and I discovered there are 2 Chaumonts in France, — one southeast and one southwest of Paris! Toward which should we go? And then we spent ¾ of an hour trying to get the right one on the phone – but no answer in either town – Blindly we chose the larger Chaumont, — and headed out of Paris!!!* —Rusty

> *So we started out thinking we would phone about 1/3 of the way along to say we might have to stop along the way for the night. Drove madly through wet autumn night hoping we'd make it in time so we wouldn't have to stay at a hotel. (Also, we were jogging way out of our way to do this since we were supposed to be heading up into Germany to the top of the Rhine.) Anyway, about 1/3 of the way there we stopped and phoned – only to find out that Rusty's friend had gone to the hospital!* —Kit

Because Rusty didn't think of giving her friend, Babe Davies, their address in Paris, Babe and her husband, Ken, were not able to contact them. When the girls finally reached Ken, they learned that, due to a stomach ulcer, Babe was in a hospital in Frankfurt and would be there for a week.

> *So there we were, miles out of our way at 9:00 p.m. in a tiny little town. Looked up my faithful Michelin Guidebook and found us a hotel nearby [Le Coq à la Poule in Provins]. Real quaint – very French country type. Grubby-ish woman with kerchief, assorted dogs, geese, and an old man with drooping yellow mustaches hovering over an immense copper kettle and sampling its steaming*

contents from time to time – these were our first impressions. Our
room turned out to be very warm and comfortable – no hot water
but tons of atmosphere. We had a snack before bed and breakfast
next morning and including tip it only cost us $0.85 each! —Kit

The girls drove through the hilly French countryside and stopped at Reims Cathedral which Kit described as "another beautiful Gothic cathedral" with "more beautiful rose windows!" Rusty described it as "in a sad state of disrepair – all the heads and arms seem to be falling off the multiple statues which decorate the exterior." Both emphasized the interior's simplicity, and Rusty described it as one of the most beautiful cathedrals she'd ever seen. "Very plain and simple; and the rose window is breath-taking – the loveliest I have ever seen!"

Rusty also noted, "A wedding was just finishing as we entered; - so we heard another boys' choir, saw a lovely bride in filmy white at the altar." Kit added, "Imagine being married on the <u>very same</u> altar where Joan of Arc crowned the Dauphin." After lunch in Reims, Kit and Rusty drove on to Luxembourg, their ninth country.

21

Losing Possessions in Luxembourg
(November 3 – November 4, 1954)

Well, it had to happen – as it does to all uninsured 26-year old,
blondish, female, blue-eyed American tourists in Luxembourg,
Europe, during the month of November – yup – I was robbed!
Imagine – me ... ! Now, Mom, stop gasping – I still have my health
and my shift [chemise] left! And my money (except about $20 worth
of foreign currency which was in my suitcase). We Tuckers seem to
have developed a penchant – or rather I should say a penchant for us
has been developed by the "breaking and entering" type. So here's
the sad story ... —Kit

After arriving in Luxembourg the night of November 3, the
girls found a room at a hotel where they spent their last night of
blissful naïveté. The next morning, Rusty wrote, "We awoke at the
usual hour (about 7:30) and were finishing packing, preparing to
leave when the phone rang and the desk girl said the Police

wanted to see Miss Tyler." Since the room was registered in Kit's name, the girls were puzzled. How did they know to ask for anyone by the name of Tyler?

"Needless to say, we hurried down," Kit wrote. They found two uniformed Luxembourg policemen waiting for them. "Went around to the hotel parking lot where Europa was – and, sure enough, it looked like she had put up a brave fight but the front window vent had been pried open and the window sash was half out."

Kit looked inside the car and discovered only two suitcases on the seat, "My carpak and Rusty's large suitcase – my blue one was gone and Rusty's plastic bag ... "

> *I was terrified to look. When they first told me our car had been broken into, — I was numb. I set my jaw and tried to shut my mind so as not to think, — but a couple of pictures did flash through – my camera which I had just put under the front seat, — and my big suitcase which held all my sweaters, skirts, wool suits, — and my Xmas presents, — That's what bothered me most ... all those things I had bought for you which I would never be able to replace! – We looked – and there in the back seat sat my big suitcase and Kit's car pack. I dived under the seat and there was my camera. Relief flooded over me – Then I heard Kit's shaken voice saying " ... suitcase ... plastic bag ... " And I [realized] that those were the only things missing. —Rusty*

"Couldn't believe it – a real weird feeling to know that most of what you possess in the world is gone," Kit wrote.

> *My blue case was the heaviest thing in the car. We kept it jammed in between the front and back seats – it was a tight squeeze and*

required lots of pulling, tugging, and maneuvering to get it out. My
carpak and Rusty's suitcase both sit on the seat and are very easy to
get at. They left our cameras in the car – these were under the front
seats so maybe they didn't see them. —Kit

With names like Trinkas and Schmidt, the police reminded the
girls of a comic operetta, but both wrote that the policemen were
very nice. The girls gave their names and addresses to the police
as well as a list of their missing possessions.

While Kit was dazed, Rusty was able to recall exactly what was
missing.

In my plastic bag were:

black winter coat;
trench coat;
striped ordon-wool dress;
zebra corduroy robe;
brown full wool skirt;
and some odds & ends that were in the bottom

"Rusty, of course, knew exactly what she had in her plastic bag,
but I was in a complete spin – couldn't seem to think of anything –
just that I had practically nothing left in the way of sweaters."
Later, Kit described her stolen items in a letter to her family:

5 cashmeres ("nope, not the gray one this time – had it on!");
raincoat ("I nearly cried on the spot when I realized it");
brand new ski sweater ("irreplaceable since I doubt if I will ever get
to Norway again and it's no fun having one you didn't buy there –
it's too bad you'll never see it – it was really gorgeous*!");*
gifts ("all the presents I had bought including many Christmas gift
type things");

black lace dress ("we really got a chuckle over that – I never did wear it and how you struggled to finish it, Mom – it's been sort of a gag with us – when day after day we wore skirts and socks and slacks and loafers, sometimes while washing up for dinner I would turn to Rusty and say languidly – "I think I'll wear my black lace tonight. So, I hope some little buxom Luxembourg belle gives it a whirl");

black sheath dress;

small black pocketbook;

evening bag;

several stoles;

red and white embroidered cotton dress;

only girdle ("can't gain an ounce now and I just started to put on a little weight too!");

three knitted suits ("dark green, beloved pink one, and the 3-piece black and blue");

all kinds [of] lingerie, towels, etc.; ("and horror of horrors – my crinoline – whatever will I do without it! Tch, tch.").

Rusty wrote:

It was a nightmare – a dream – This wasn't real – not happening to us! The police told us what had happened as much as they knew: — Another couple in the hotel had packed up their car, then gone to have breakfast (as we were about in the process of doing); — they came back out to their car about 8:45 and discovered their car had been robbed. They called the police and the police then made a check of all the cars which were parked in the hotel private parking lot (near the street) and then discovered our car. They found 2 suitcases belonging to the other couple, which apparently had been dropped in haste. – They are fairly sure the thieves are some young boys.

—Rusty

With instructions to come to Police Headquarters at noon, the girls walked back up to their room in a haze. According to Rusty:

> *Half an hour and the phone rang again. — Downstairs a big burly plain-clothesman blustering his German language marched us back out to Europa. We stood there shivering while he sprinkled fingerprint powder about the window and the doors; — decided the boys must have been wearing gloves – no fingerprints.*

> *At 12:00 noon we stood in the office at Police Headquarters while 4 policemen exploded German at each other and another (Schmidt) interpreted for us. We gave them as detailed a list as possible of all the things we were missing. They kept us here for some time and then showed us where the Renault garage was so we could get Europa fixed.* —Rusty

The girls drove Europa to a Renault garage only to discover that the garage was closed from 12:00 – 2:00.

> *(In France, too, there is a 2 hour lunch period for <u>everyone</u>. Even big dept. stores <u>LOCK UP</u> between those hours – <u>Everything</u> stops for lunch.) Our gas gauge had registered empty for a long time – but we had no Luxembourg money and only 10 francs (20 cents) in Belgian money (which they accept and use, too).* —Rusty

"So there we were," Kit wrote.

> *Couldn't leave the car there and couldn't buy any gas and didn't have enough gas in the tank to drive back into the city and around. Looked at the man helplessly – explained our predicament – he asked how much change we had in Luxembourg money – we counted – about 10 francs ($.20). He said fine, he'd give us 10 francs worth (about 2 quarts) and then we would be able to drive into the city and*

*back at 1:30. So we did. Imagine an American gas station attendant selling you $.20 worth of gas! —*Kit

"So between 2:00 and 4:00 we left Europa to be fixed, and then walked and walked; — trying to get our minds back in focus; — Hadn't had anything much to eat so stopped for some hot tea, which warmed our stomachs and our souls." Rusty wrote:

*Walked into the Police station again promptly at 4:00, and there on the desk lay my plastic bag!!!! I hurriedly unzipped it and took quick inventory to discover that my two coats were gone, — they had removed those but left the dress, skirt, and my robe which had been hanging underneath. In his broken English the Head policeman said the plastic bag had been found near the car! — Am sick; — but must remember: that it could have been so much worse; — Feel terribly sorry for Kit; — she has her car pack which contains her skirts and slacks and one good dress; — the skirt, 2 shirts, and the sweater she was wearing! All her other clothes are gone, — plus all the things she had collected along the way – her ski sweater, — ad infinitum — And she has no insurance. I'm afraid there is no hope of getting anything more back. Though we are to go back to the Police again tomorrow morning . —*Rusty

Kit wrote:

*But still no trace of my suitcase and if they haven't got it by now it's either at the bottom of the river or on its way to East Siberia! After this we dropped over to the American [Embassy] just to let them know. Man was very friendly – first case like this he'd ever had in Luxembourg – wouldn't ya know – it hadda be us! I arranged to have the police contact them if there are any developments after I leave and they said they would phone every other day for several weeks just to keep on top of it. —*Kit

Rusty wrote:

We have taken ourselves in hand, are trying to be good Pollyannas, are saying things like "What's done is done," — "no use crying over spoiled milk," — "It could have been so much worse, — we're lucky" — "Worrying and fretting are not going to bring it back" – and we are braving up admirably. —Rusty

Fortunately for Rusty, her mother had convinced her to purchase personal insurance as well as car insurance. Kit, however, did not have insurance. Rusty wrote:

We collected our money from the insurance company for our broken windshield in Paris only 2 days ago and now tomorrow I must go to the agent here in Luxembourg and try to collect for our damaged window. There is no agent for my personal insurance between here and Genova, Italy, so I'm going to write a letter to the London agent. Wonder how long it will take for me to collect the money for the coat. … Good thing it's so warm – and that we're heading for Italy. I had worn my trench coat so much, — I had to have it cleaned in London; - then decided to keep it clean and save it for special days and moments. — Too bad, wish I hadn't decided that! My faithful old green corduroy coat is still with me – And only minutes before it happened, I had decided to wear my green leather jacket, so had taken it out of the plastic bag. – Thank heavens, because they would surely have kept that! —Rusty

Kit tried to cheer up her parents:

So that's the end of my little story for the day. Don't worry and fret – I'll be fine – just traveling light and that'll be good experience. You, I almost didn't write and tell you and then I had a vision of me getting off the boat and Daddy saying "Where's your blue suitcase?" and me having to explain right then and there. It would spoil the big homecoming so I wrote all the gory details and now we can forget about it – I have to. If I moaned and groaned it wouldn't get me anywhere and would only spoil our trip so we're throwing all kinds of Pollyanna and "material things don't matter" and "what's done is done" and "don't cry over … etc." at each other – and so I think we'll pull through. For a while it'll be a little tough as I discover one by one all the little things that are gone – but so be it. We're really lucky they didn't take everything! Also – just think when I get home I'll have to go out and buy almost ¾ of a complete wardrobe – all at once – what fun! It's always been one of my lifelong ambitions to go out and buy all my clothes at once – sort of a grand spree – and now I'll be forced to - sounds wonderful!   —Kit

Germany, Austria and Switzerland

The moon came up, and with almost a frightened start we realized that the silver full moon was not peering behind a dark cloud, but rather that was a gigantic mountain ahead of us!!!

~Rusty Tyler

22

Clinking in Germany
(November 5 – November 10, 1954)

The robbery was crushing, but Rusty and Kit didn't let it get them down. They shook it off, collected themselves, and got back on the road. They headed out of Luxembourg and into Germany, ready for more positive adventures.

Rusty later said, "We came to the German border. We had to stop. My goodness out came those Germans. They clicked their heels and saluted. It really put the fear of God in you. It was scary because it was right after the war and the Nazis."

Back on September 27, the girls had spent one night in Germany on their way from The Netherlands to Denmark. At the time, Rusty noted that the beds were comfortable and had promised to describe them to her mother in more detail after they returned. She took the opportunity to do so on November 11:

Most of them are built kind of like hospital beds; — they have the head section of the mattress raised slightly. There is a lightly stretched sheet over the mattress; and the pillow is <u>gigantic</u> – <u>square</u>, (<u>red</u> – with white pillowcase), and filled with <u>down</u>; — and <u>then</u>: — for the covering there is a <u>large</u> Eiderdown comforter … not quilted in any way – just this huge thing, fluffy as can be, and a case (like a giant pillowcase) is its covering, — snapping shut at the one end. That's all you have to put over you. … No other sheet or blanket or anything – But it's warmer than 50 blankets! Once you get in bed, the whole thing begins to warm up and pretty soon it's like you were in a toasty little oven. I love them!! Would <u>love</u> to bring some home and use them! —Rusty

The following day, November 6, after one night in Koblenz, Germany, Rusty and Kit drove along the Rhine River towards Frankfurt. The weather was uncooperative, and therefore, the views were less than spectacular. However, they did see a lot of vineyards, and Rusty's description of them in her letter home painted a vivid picture:

We were enchanted by the vineyards which covered for miles the hillsides. And dotted here and there were men and women out picking the grapes. The men all wore large cone shaped baskets on their backs; the women all were dressed in full dirndl skirts, aprons, and kerchiefs. … Some of the hills had many "levels;" – with about 3 ft. high brick "walls" to hold the soil and keep it from being washed down; — These walls laced the hills … and the grape vines which train around sticks are all cut off short … no higher than 3 or 4 feet. (I had always pictured a vineyard to be almost like a grape arbor – such a surprise!) —Rusty

The girls reached Wiesbaden around 1:00 p.m. They were hoping to find Babe Davies, the friend of Rusty's they had been planning to visit in Chaumont. Rusty wrote:

> *Ken Davies had told me that Babe was in Hospital 7100; — this was Greek to me, and Wiesbaden is a pretty big place, so I really had very little hopes of ever succeeding in seeing her. – But as we were driving in, suddenly Kit exclaimed "There's 7100!" – And there was a sign for 7100 USAF Hosp. – So, we followed that and several more signs, and came driving into the grounds of a GIGANTIC hospital. – Suddenly we became terribly excited – and we could hardly contain ourselves as we saw American Air Force men walking around! –The first Americans we had seen for a long time – and as we saw their jaunty walk and overheard the old familiar American slang we wanted to run up and kiss every one of them!!! We found the Information desk right away, asked where Mrs. Regina Davies was and the man gave us the directions – right up on the 3rd floor; — so up we went, and was Babe ever surprised!*
> *—Rusty*

While visiting Babe in the hospital, Rusty mentioned that they were expecting to see Mary and Harry Sommers (mutual friends from South Dakota) in Frankfurt. Babe encouraged them to give the Sommers a call right then from the hospital, which they did. Mary and Harry were both home and insisted that the girls come on over. Kit described their visit in her journal:

> *He is a Major in the Army – a warrant officer. We are staying tonight and tomorrow night. They have a <u>fabulous</u> apartment. It is absolute <u>heaven</u>! Huge steak for dinner. Having a wonderful time! Went to a nightclub – all Americans – It's on the post. Just like home. Oh, they have a 2 door Ford with plastic roof – weirdest*

feeling – car seems <u>immense</u> – like a boat – after Europa. I'll <u>never</u>
be able to drive one! —Kit

Rusty elaborated on their first night with Mary and Harry:

Mary put us in this lovely big bedroom and she was a very
charming hostess. Kit and I <u>delighted</u> in <u>spreading</u> <u>out</u> – And in
robes and slippers we curled up on the davenport and had canapes
and talked. Oh yes, and they have a maid, too; — Tilly, a wonderful
German girl, who speaks very good English, is friendly and fun –
certainly is a <u>gem</u> for Mary. – We had a magnificent dinner!
Gigantic <u>T-Bone</u> steaks, avocado salad, French-fried potatoes, and
Brussel sprouts. – And hard crusted poppy seed <u>German</u> rolls –
And black coffee (No dessert).

Then we hurried to get dressed up as Harry had made reservations
for us at the Casino, — a room in the Officers' Club – It used to
belong to the Germans and was an officers' club for the Nazis! –
Kept trying to imagine what it was like over 10 years ago – and who
the people were who were sitting where we were sitting.

Harry slyly invited 2 very handsome young men who were looking
very "alone" at a nearby table to join us. One was Jack – and one
was Hardy Glasgow, — and I must say, I was quite attracted to this
particular one! – And, I believe, he to me – (ha!) – Anyway, we all
six talked like crazy! – Jack and Hardy were 2nd Lieuts. in the Air
Force, — they fly jet planes. —Rusty

The next day the girls slept late at Mary and Harry's and
enjoyed a wonderful "American" style breakfast, which Rusty
detailed. "Fresh orange juice (the first I'd had since I left the good
old USA, fruit juice is not very popular over here, and most of the
orange juice I've had has been that acid canned variety), — 2 fried

eggs, bacon; hot crisp toast, grape jam, hot coffee cake, and coffee."

After breakfast, they all took a drive along the Rhine River. Rusty wrote home about the day, starting with a description of the monument known as the Watch on the Rhine:

Das Nationaldenkmal auf dem Niederwald

Postcard, mailed home by Rusty, of the Watch on the Rhine.

[…] A gigantic statue depicting the "mother" of Germany, built by Bismarck at the end of the Franco-Prussian War to symbolize Germany's rise again. The statue is large and war-like – she's frightening just to look at her. – And at her feet she has a statue of a

*man symbolizing war at her right, and at her left a statue
symbolizing peace. ... They all looked very warlike to me! A massive
thing – and looking out far across the Rhine. As Harry says, they
need another one facing the other way now — (towards Russia). –*

*Drove down beside the Rhine again to the Lorelei Rock. ... And we
had Sunday dinner in a little restaurant right there. Delicious
German food, served family style: I had schweinebraten (pork,
roasted and cooked in a delicious sauce); browned potatoes, lightly
creamed peas and carrots, — strange, flavorful soups, and large
pieces of rye bread. Stewed pears for dessert.*

*That was our furthest point, and then we started back, passing
through quaint little German villages – and gazing up after at the
many many medieval castles that overlook the Rhine. Some are still
being occupied –as homes! And some are museums and one we
discovered was a girls' school; — that one was built on such a high
rocky point, they must have to bring up the girls in baskets! – It
must be almost like a prison up there! – Dark and gloomy. —
Intriguing looking, though. –*

*On our way across country, we suddenly found ourselves driving
into a street of gay laughing boisterous crowds and brightly colored
lights, — A carnival! With the help of 2 German policemen, Harry
finally got the Ford parked near a filling station, and we all trouped
out to enter a German Carnival! — All along the street were cotton
candy stands, "hot-dog" stands (only you should see those hot dogs!
About one and a half inches thick, and eight inches long, and more
the color of a sausage than our weiners. – Too bad we were so full –
I would like to have tried one!) Did buy some hot, freshly crispy –
caramel coated almonds! Mmmmm were they delicious! They had
many different kinds of strange looking candy, etc. – People were*

milling about, very happy and gay and noisy – Old old men, thin
and stooped, with their long bushy moustaches; and old old women,
plump, and wearing black long coats and a black kerchief tied under
their chins. – Strong young farmers rosy-cheeked and devilish-eyed
– Sturdy blond girls, laughing and flirting – Elfin children dressed
in their hand-knit leggings, sweaters and stocking caps, — looking
like they were over-sized Xmas tree ornaments; — A merry-go-
round, a motor-car-bumper, a strange variation of the "bullet" –
dart-tossing, ring-throwing, — Harry shot a gun and won a funny
paper corsage of flowers for Mary; — Mary took chances on a
gigantic display of fancy gifts and won the typical cheap objects and
gave them to a little boy – a fun-house brought forth hearty German
ejaculations and screaming laughter, — Two American soldiers
(privates) stood conspicuously by, watching everything a little
longingly. – Stands for selling lace, pottery, brushes, hardware, etc.
littered the streets; a magician pulled rabbits from a hat; and a
*barker was selling his patented medicine … —*Rusty

After witnessing the life that Harry and Mary were leading, both girls became interested in getting a job with the Army. Kit noted the government was starting a new TV station and that they might try to get jobs there. Rusty wrote to her mother:

Kit and I have decided that to work for the Army is the only thing to
do!!! Their privileges and extra benefits are absolutely fabulous!
Just a few of the things: (1) The PX, which is almost like Marshall
Fields – everything you can imagine, — and sold at ridiculous low
prices! For instance, a German camera might cost $150.00 in the
States; in Germany it would cost $100.00 and in the PX $75.00 —
some of the things are almost absurd! All their mail is mailed with
USA postage and is charged only from New York to destinations –

across the ocean it's free. No duty to pay on any imported articles, either!

At special filling stations gas costs 15¢ a gallon for all Army personnel. – In Germany we paid 63¢ a gallon!!! There are many big resort hotels throughout Germany (especially in Garmisch, and in the German Alps) that belonged to the Germans and ordinarily, would cost about $15.00 to $20.00 a day, — the soldiers can stay there for $1.50 a day. And there are Mediterranean cruises and tours which are arranged for Army personnel at some fantastically unbelievable low prices!! And I could go on and on.

Of course, Harry Sommers is a major, — but I wish you could see their apt.! – Spacious, lovely, beautifully furnished – I think Mary said they pay $150.00 for it — And according to N.Y. standards that apt. would rent for $400.00 cheap; would probably be a lot more!   —Rusty

The next day Kit wrote in her journal:

Slept late again – yummy! Had breakfast on little table by big window – served by Tilly – Mary & Harry's wonderful German maid. Such a life! Rusty was very sick last night – I was quite worried but she felt much better this morning. Went to the PX center with Mary. Had <u>delicious</u> hamburger and a chocolate malt. Tasted superb. Sat in the cafeteria while Mary shopped. Had a marvelous time looking at all the Americans – <u>love 'em!</u> This occupation army really has a deal! Wouldn't mind being attached to it myself – The PX alone is worth its weight in gold – they get anything from a pair of I. Miller shoes to a pop-up toaster at a fantastic price plus all the native products too. And the fabulous advantage of being over and being able to see so many things and

places. Mary very kindly bought us a bunch of necessities at the PX.
—Kit

Rusty was a little more forthright about the "necessities" that Mary bought for them in the PX, though she still did not spell it out completely:

While Kit and I sipped coffee, Mary shopped in the PX for us (we aren't even allowed beyond the <u>door</u>!) — she bought us kleenex, k---x, shampoo, film (at $4.65 for me), twine and tissue paper, alka seltzer, aspirin, — etc. – What a savings for us! Kit had bought a small box of kleenex in France for $1.00!! Can you imagine?! More errands and a quick tour of the Army bldgs. – and home. —Rusty

The following day they left the home of Mary and Harry and drove on to Heidelberg, a picturesque university town, well known for the castle of the same name that overlooks it. When they checked in at American Express, there was big news as reported in Kit's journal:

Letter from Chris! Said he "found he missed me quite a lot" in typical surprised British fashion. Said it was up to me about Italy. Don't know what the devil to do – I would like to see him again but I hate to be the one to take the initiative – Damn it – probably will never see him again. ... —Kit

At Heidelberg Castle, as they were waiting under an arcade for the rain to stop, the girls met Private Herm Grabert and Private Barnett "Bunny" Fair. Kit called them "very entertaining!" in her journal. Herm was a baseball player for the St. Louis Cardinals, and Bunny was a ballet fan who visited City Center and had a girl [girlfriend] in South Orange, New Jersey – "small world" wrote

Kit. They had a beer and sandwich at the Red Ox Inn together, and Kit wrote in her journal of the plans they made:

> They talked us into going to Stuttgart and Munich so we could be in Zurich by Saturday when they might have a weekend pass. Elaborate plans for contacting – (leave message at Cross Roads – etc) – probably never work out but we had a wonderful time all the same. Staying at freezing cold tiny hotel – almost couldn't get in after paying our money at the Tourist office! Rang and rang bell – finally went in through door - old woman – no speak English – oi voy anyway we're here!   Kit

The old woman who spoke no English was a favorite of Kit's. The next day Kit wrote in her journal about her, "Woman at hotel a riot. Took a shine to us – didn't want us [to] leave – thought it so funny we couldn't speak German – laughed and laughed and enjoyed tremendously – kept putting her arm around us – holding our hands – just a character."

Rusty wrote home about her as well, describing her as red nosed with gray fuzzy hair. "She didn't want us to leave Stuttgart yet; and she kept holding my hand, and then throwing her arms around me and <u>laughing</u> — such heartiness – such warmth!"

In addition to the woman at the hotel, Stuttgart was remembered as a town where they left a lot of money behind. While doing a little shopping, the girls were lured into a photography shop. In 1954, digital cameras did not exist and 35mm cameras were not the norm, but Rusty loved to take photographs. She wrote:

> Guess what? I bought a self-timer for about $2.50, a wonderful tripod for $7.00, a haze filter for about $2.00, and a wonderful light

meter for $15.00!! It's a German make and it's automatic — It's cream colored; I bought a leather case for it so it's on my camera strap; and all I do is turn a little dial to the numbers of my film rating, (it will probably never be changed now as I always use the same: Kodachrome). Then I hold it toward my subject, press in a little button, hold for a couple of seconds, - release, and there it is!! The exact reading I should set it for! I love it!! —Rusty

Rusty wrote about Kit's big purchase after she listed all the photographic equipment she herself had bought.

Kit got completely carried away, and she bought a <u>camera</u>!! Steve White had given her a new Ansco for her birthday last summer, — but it's not 35 mm; and she wants to have colored slides, so — she bought a new Agfa for only $20.00!! It's a brand new camera - has only been on the market four months – Has 3.5 – 16 [mm] lens (same as mine), shutter speed of 25 to 200 – (mine has 10-200), a very clever fast spring lock which winds the film to the next picture frame, locks the "trigger," and a self timer that's built in to the camera!! – Really is a dandy; — and for that price it's fabulous! —Rusty

They drove on to Munich that day and called Sumner Ghimschu, someone they had worked with at NBC who now worked for Radio Free Europe, and arranged to meet him for drinks and dinner. Rusty wrote home about their first day with Sumner. She was captivated by the places he took them. It is a long passage but one that deserves to be read in its entirety:

In the outskirts of town, we stopped at a phone booth, — experimented and luckily hit the jackpot and got Radio Free Europe, and – *Sumner Ghimschu* — *Both Kit and I knew him very well at NBC – and a year ago last summer he told us we'd never go to Europe – it was just a fancy and we didn't have the "whatever it takes" to go. — He was teasing but also serious – And then this summer he quit NBC and got a job with Radio Free Europe – And here we all three were in* <u>Munich</u>*!! Made arrangements to meet him at 6:00 – so then we made our way through* <u>startling</u> *Munich traffic (it was almost worse than Paris!) and found a hotel. – Dressed and met Sumner – it seemed soooo funny to be seeing him in Germany!! – He took us to Humpelmayr, one of the most famous and best restaurants in Munich, and we sat at a small table in a cozy gay, room —- soft lights, exciting people, soft carpets, and an orchestra of a piano, guitar, violin, and accordion, and they played lovely* <u>German</u> *music, folk, operatic, and semi-classical –* <u>Delightful</u>*!!! I had* <u>venison</u> *broiled with a slice of pineapple and a dark cherry on top; a rich brown cream sauce was poured over that – wonderful delicate flavor! Beside the venison was a mound of juicy red berries; — and a mound of buttery German noodles (that look and taste home-made) was served with this. – Quite delicious! — Oh yes, and before this we had consomme served with rings of tiny sausages floating in it.* —Rusty

Rusty later said, "The men waiting on us were all in white and very formal. I was dying of thirst. No one gave you water! I did not drink wine. Kit did. I kept saying, 'Can I have a glass of water?' They kept smiling and nodding and never did. At the end of the meal they brought a big platter of grapes and a glass of water. I was so excited. I drank all the water then looked around and realized others were dipping their grapes in the water. I was mortified."

After soaking in lots of this fine German atmosphere we were escorted in Sumner's Chevrolet to the Officers' Club of Munich – (he, by working for RFE has many Army privileges) – We drove up beside a block long white stone bldg. with Greek columns from one end to the other … an attractive and very interesting building. The name of it is the Haus der Kunst, – and this was also one of Hitler's "hangouts" – using it, I believe, in much the same way that the Americans are using it now. – Inside it's lovely. – Sumner showed us around the main floor first: — the bar and lounge, the large plush dining room, a "writing room" and lounge, — and the dance "hall" – We stayed in the latter, sitting at a white linened table and had coffee and apple strudel for dessert. A large 16 piece orchestra (German) was playing American dance music, and the atmosphere was soft and inviting –

From there Sumner took us to the Hofbrauhaus which is something I have heard so much about and had been very anxious to see! It's the largest and most famous beer hall in the world, and another of Hitler's favorite places. This is where he used to come and meet with all his cronies, have fanatic meetings, much gaiety, and get drunk. I had pictured it as more of a rathskeller type, — like the Red Ox Inn in Heidlelberg only larger – As we came to the door and walked in I was shocked! It was like a gigantic cave. long unfinished wooden tables filled with men (of the real working class), lush blonde waitresses serving huge stone steins of beer (each mug holds a quart of beer!) ice cold; — it's big and heavy … Groups of men singing boisterous German songs, — a perfect setting for Hitler and his beginning of Nazism. … I was shocked and I was thrilled and I was entranced – I had never seen anything to compare with this –

*The floor is of gray stone and the immense room is filled with low "archways" in crumbling yellow plaster, which gives you the feeling that you are almost walking in an underground cave. Only beer is served as I gazed wide-eyed and silent while Sumner ordered beer for Kit and himself. And they each get these stone mugs holding a <u>quart</u> of icy beer. <u>Pretzels</u> the size of a pie-plate were served – Near the front door there was a small counter where all kinds of German beer steins were sold. I couldn't resist, so I bought a smaller model of the ones used in the Hofbrauhaus. It's sort of blended grayish bluish whitish and has a big HB and small "insignia" on it. —*Rusty

While in Munich, Rusty wrote home about the presents she was sending:

A couple of things: Mary got me a large box and gave me Xmas seals and wrapping etc. And she packed your Xmas box for me, and Harry took it down and mailed it for me; — and <u>paid</u> for the postage, — wouldn't let me give him a cent. – And you see they can mail it from the PX and only have to pay postage from <u>New York</u> to <u>South Dakota</u> ....But that's a <u>secret</u>. – And so it had to have Major Sommer's return address on it. – Don't tell anybody, tho, cause they're not supposed to mail things for other people. So tickled though, — and grateful! And then Harry wouldn't even let me pay for the N.Y. to S.D. postage! When you get it, open it; — inside there is a present for Clayton, — one for Rex; — and one for Alicejo. Because of weight, <u>nothing</u> is in a box, — and it's wrapped only in white tissue paper; — so – no "feeling" please! <u>And</u> no peeking!! PLEASE!!!! You <u>have</u> to save it for Christmas! There are several <u>tiny</u> packages for you, so be careful you don't throw any of them away in the packing!

Then – in Heidleberg I bought 2 other things and had them mailed. Be sure and let me know as soon as the box arrives, — but don't open it, as I don't think they will be gift wrapped inside. — Here's a clue for one thing: the time is "I Lost My Heart in Heidelberg," – love the song! And Heidleberg is a delightful city! We loved it, too! He he – curious?!

Will find something soon for Charles [Rusty's future step-father] and will have it mailed from the store (I have an idea). ...

I love Germany! It's a beautiful country! – And the people are very friendly and on the most part, quite warm to us. I was surprised, really. Details soon, I promise! —Rusty

The next day Rusty and Kit met Sumner at the Officers' Club for lunch. Then they went to Radio Free Europe for a job interview. Kit summed up the result in her journal, "Nothing doing – damn it! Rusty is going to have a hard time without shorthand. Said goodbye to Sumner – a nice guy – tried hard for us."

Drove out of Munich with its bustling city life, new modern bldgs. booming reconstruction; — its shell-like museums, theatres, churches, — rubble-filled with their interiors completely bombed out — Germany makes you so much more conscious of War, past and foreboding future, than any other country. The German people are remarkable – staunch, strong and determined, they have bounded back with fantastic speed and Germany is a modern fast-moving up-to-date country! —Rusty

The girls drove on that day, and in a letter home Rusty described the scenery along the way, from Munich through southern Germany to Innsbruck, Austria:

From Munich we drove through rolling green hills, dotted with clusters of black-green pine trees, gaily colored German farms neatly plowed fields, — and completing the perfect picture were men pushing their plows behind large work horses, their breaths steaming in the cold crisp air. Along the road we passed men pulling cart loads of green hay. ...

Southern Germany is really a lovely country! – And then twilight, a beautiful sunset, and it was night with a million stars twinkling above us – The moon came up, and with almost a frightened start we realized that the silver full moon was not peering behind a dark cloud, but rather that was a gigantic mountain ahead of us!!! And soon we were surrounded by high black mountains, their snow-capped peaks silver in the moonlight. Awesome and mysteriously beautiful. — We wound round and round at their base, driving through adorable mountain villages that were filled with hotels and ski lodges and gay sports shops. After Garmisch (main resort for US soldiers now) we began climbing – up and down and around – Bright moonlight, and twinkling lights of a village at the side of a moon – shimmering lake. Climbed some terribly high mountains and then almost straight down with signs along the road saying "Low gear" and with a skull and crossbones above that. – Cheery thought. —Rusty

23

Clambering in Austria
(November 11 – November 13, 1954)

The girls passed quickly through Austria and Liechtenstein, staying only one night in each country. Kit had this to say about their lodgings in Innsbruck, Austria:

> *In wonderful hotel – terribly modern and luxurious. About $1.17 + 15% service – __very__ good! Turned out to be one of the hotels mentioned in Rusty's guidebook – never would have come in if we had known – look what we would have missed.* —Kit

The girls woke up the next morning in Innsbruck to a beautiful day. They took a cable car up Hafelekar Mountain, located at 2300 meters above sea level. Kit wrote in her journal that she "took pictures like mad." Rusty did as well, and wrote to her mother:

> *The VIEW!!! Took several pictures (so glad I had my new haze filter!) Wore my ski sweater and was warmer than toast! Then we clambered down, sat in the lodge for a few moments, and took the next cable car down to where we changed, but stayed on at the large*

lodge there — Marvelous view, and we had weiner schnitzel and delicious lunch in a rustic dining room; — copper pots hung on the wooden beams along the walls, and ivy was growing up the walls and across the ceiling!! We were next to the large windows which looked out over a green valley far below, the tiny model city of Innsbruck, and gigantic rocky peaks across from us.

The night grew very black before the moon could climb above the high mountains but when it did it bathed everything in silver again. Lovely lovely Austria. Crossed the border into Liechtenstein about 8:00. ... I must admit, I never realized it was a country, before!!!
—Rusty

Kit and I on top of Alps — Innsbruck. —Rusty

Rusty and Kit had little to say about Austria but even less to say about Liechtenstein, the eleventh country on their trip. They stayed in a town called Vaduz. The next day, they got up early and continued on to Switzerland.

24

Lingering in Lucerne
(November 13 – November 17, 1954)

Unlike Austria and Liechtenstein, Rusty and Kit spent considerably longer in their next country – Switzerland. They stayed five nights in three different cities. The girls were off to a good start with a beautiful drive from Vaduz, Liechtenstein, to Zurich, Switzerland. On November 13, Kit wrote in her journal:

> *Gorgeous drive! Indescribable! Took a picture of a lovely mountain village with a gleaming copper steeple on its church. Also took one of a miniature castle and village on somebody's front lawn! Saw a house – just started – with a little fir tree attached to the front roof decorated with men's hankies – must be a custom!* —Kit

"Zurich is a very pretty city," Rusty wrote. "Much flatter than I had imagined it would be. The Alps look very distant, and the city is spread out around the end of a large blue lake. The traffic was wild here, too at first."

Rusty standing next to Europa in Zurich.

Just made it to Amexco in time to pick up message from Bunny &
Herm [two men they'd met in Heidelberg]. Then we waited an hour
at the prescribed time in front of Amexco and they never arrived!
Just sick – they probably got tied up or something – damn it. Was
really looking forward to it! Went to Eng movie – nice little usher
gave us wonderful seats – much better than we bought! —Kit

The movie was *Innocents in Paris* and was in English with
German and French subtitles. The girls were very tickled because
they could "identify every scene and background" in the movie.

Earlier that day, on the way to Zurich, the girls got a flat tire. It
was their first one of the trip, and Kit noted that they were very
lucky because it happened in a small town just down the road
from a huge Esso station:

I ran down the road to the station and upon arriving, discovered I
had left the little phrase book in the car – sooo – with graphic

gestures, I described a flat tire – everybody laughed – and a young man and I started off up the road. It took him about 2 minutes to fix it. Change it, that is, and we were off again. I can see what would have happened if we had been on one of those lonely mountain roads when it happened! Rusty and I have been meaning to have a session with the French jack but haven't done so as yet. Like most French mechanical gadgets, it is quite baffling looking. The little man at the Renault agency did explain it to us when we first got the car – but like most French explanations of mechanical gadgets, it too was rather baffling – in fact, completely so! —Kit

Rusty wrote home that they were hurrying to get to Zurich before the American Express closed at noon. This reminded her to explain to her mother that military time was used everywhere in Europe.

By the way, I guess I forgot to mention that in Europe the time is from 1:00 to 24:00 o'clock!! Since the war, every country has adapted this system. At first we nearly went crazy with signs being posted such as POST OFFICE OPEN: 8:30 – 12:00 and 14:00 – 18:30 and Box Office opens at 20:30 – And the other day we saw a clock: Everyone seems very happy with it and all agree that it's much more efficient and logical and why didn't they do it long ago? —Rusty

The next day Kit wrote that it was another beautiful day and that they "Bumped into [usher] from the movies last night! Right next to our hotel – he really was so nice." After touring around Zurich admiring the varied architecture, they drove on to Lucerne in the afternoon passing hundreds of "brown Swiss cows with huge cowbells hanging round their necks." Once they reached Lucerne, Kit reported that they found a "lovely room in the

Montrose hotel overlooking the lake – with shower (and a marvelous one too!)" Rusty gave the folks back home a vivid picture of Lucerne:

Our first glimpse of Lucerne completely enchanted us and it was as if we were in a fairy tale the rest of the time we were there! A lovely lovely wonderful city!! Our hotel was in the very center of town and right on the silver-like inlet of the lake! Will mail you a postcard – look at it well, — but you cannot imagine the charm that the city has until you've been there on a Sunday afternoon in the middle of November with the low sun tinting everything a soft golden hue; when the fathers and the mothers and the little woolen-clad children are strolling about the tiny streets and tiny "platzes," lingering by the side of the water to watch the graceful white swans making lovely patterns in the water, surrounded by proud drakes and little brown mallards, strange little black birds with white beaks that emitted piquant cries, and myriads of graceful white winged birds that looked like sea-gulls swooping and diving over and down to the water. — Old men and little old ladies sat on small wooden benches and basked in the Sunday peacefulness; little Heidis threw bread crumbs into the water and laughed as the swans and the ducks competed for a piece of rather soggy bread. – Wooden covered walking bridges cross the water; one has hanging from its roof beams lovely oil paintings telling the history of Lucerne; — the other has paintings of the Dance of Death. ... Lucerne is a city of hotels, — hotels with little towers and balconies and interesting colorful scenes painted on their front walls; ... of churches – churches with tall slim spires, needle-painting the sky; ... and of clocks – clocks in every dome and steeple – red ones, blue ones, yellow ones –

Standing by the bridge, watching people feeding the swans; with church bells tolling, and the lights just starting to come on at twilight, I felt completely at peace. ... A feeling I have longed for so many, many times. Lucerne is enchantment.

This is one place you and I must go. Would give anything if you could have been with me ... thought of you so much that afternoon!
—Rusty

Rusty concluded the letter:

And I guess maybe that's all for now. – Whew! Just realized that at the top of this page I have written Page #22 — Are you exhausted, too??!! – I'll never get behind again. I promise! —Rusty

Then it was on to Interlaken and the American Express office where Kit found a much-appreciated letter from her father. "Home was beginning to seem a long way away." She continued:

Rusty and I got a big charge out of the cartoon. When it first fell out of the letter I surprised Rusty and several bystanders by exclaiming "Good grief! My father's gone on the wagon!" Anyway – glad to know The New Yorker has not folded without me – and glad to know I can still have a "bourbon on-the" with you as soon as I get home. —Kit

Around this time money was getting tight for both Rusty and Kit. Kit was looking into booking her passage home from Italy and was not finding what she hoped. There was nothing convenient from Italy. Everything was quite expensive. She wrote in her journal:

Absolutely nothing sailing from Italy damn it – Now I'll have to travel all the way up to Le Havre to sail. Going to cost <u>thousands</u> of

dollars – don't know if I'll have enough. Plane fare at cheapest is
$360 – impossible! Very depressing. —Kit

Meanwhile, the weather had become colder. They stayed at the Bahnhof Hotel in Interlaken, which Kit described as "very warm and cozy."

The plan for the day in Interlaken had been to go up Jungfrau, one of the highest peaks in Switzerland, but there was only one train a day, and it left at 8:55 a.m. Rusty and Kit woke up too late to catch it. After many vows to get up earlier the next day, they took a bus up the Niederhorn, a smaller peak, and spent the day in Beatenberg, which Rusty described as "a small Swiss village of quaint chalets built on the side and edges of the Mt." Rusty wrote that the train ride up was breathtaking, and that "the world about us looked like it was all sprinkled with powdered sugar." When the girls arrived in Beatenberg, they discovered that the chairlift to the top of the Niederhorn operated only on Sunday.

> *So we marched up and down, climbing over fences, sitting in snow banks, etc. –trying to get some pretty pictures of the mts. and views, and of the streets and people and chalets in the village. Freezing cold we finally tore ourselves away from beauty and camera and had a ham sandwich and a pot of tea. – The village really was a perfect one – each house a chalet, with the overhanging eaves, the first story painted white or tan or pink, and the top story painted or stained dark brown.*
>
> *Snow dotted everything – each house and each store had its little house for storing chopped wood, — and ears of orange corn hung from the eaves to dry. – Have never been anywhere before where it*

was so quiet. – The still crisp winter air on a bright sunny day –
occasionally an old man would come walking or riding by on his
bicycle – squeaking the snow underfoot, — or someone's voice
would ring out, — but there was a bright stillness that sort of
sparkled quietly. —Rusty

A short bit in Kit's journal from that day revealed a less
glamorous side of traveling around Europe – having to worry
about money. "Money situation – getting pretty tight – poor Rusty
even worse off than I! Very depressing again! Ate in our room."

The next day got off to a much better start. Kit did not have
much to say about the train ride up Jungfrau, but she did have a
lot to say about a gentleman they met in the hotel that morning.
She wrote about the brief encounter in her journal:

Up early – very cold! Met the greatest guy in our hotel this
morning – name of Dave Kingston. Works for Esso Standard
(Jersey) in Turkey. Noticed him as soon as I walked into breakfast –
big, red beard, mustache, reddish blond semi-crew cut, glasses. He
spoke to us at breakfast. Seemed nice. He was going up Jungfrau too
but getting on at different station. We got the car drove madly over
to our station – almost missed the train! Met Dave again – spent
entire rest of day and dinner with him. He is just marvelous – A
geologist! Imagine! Typical outdoor, pipe smoking, wonderful
stories to tell about everywhere he's been – very outgoing – likes
opera too – He met another geologist (formerly with Esso – middle-
aged man name of Pike) on the train and the two of them had us
fascinated with the conversation – so interesting. They really love
their work – and it is important – so different from the lollygags in
N.Y. Rusty and I decided we would like to marry someone like that
– Pike's wife is an English woman – very sweet and right up on

everything her husband does —with him all the time. They are
wonderful together! —Kit

Dave Kingston at Jungfrau. — Rusty

For three and a half hours, the girls and Dave rode the train up
the mountain to Jungfraujoch, which at 11,332 feet above sea level,
is Europe's highest railway station and hotel and is set down
between the two peaks of the Jungfrau. As they stepped off the
train, the white snow nearly blinded them. Rusty wrote, "Such
fierce white snow; and there were the two peaks of the Jungfrau,
rugged, foreboding, with white snow being caught and swirled
around their peaks – and the most vivid blue sky you can possibly
imagine!!"

An elevator took the girls up a level where they walked
through a long icy tunnel to view the ice sculptures in the Ice
Palace before enjoying lunch in the dining room of "thick gruyere
cheese sandwiched between dark heavy bread, and cups of
steaming chocolate. Basked in the hot sun pouring in the

windows." Warmed up, the girls took another elevator to the "sphinx," which, according to Rusty, was a lookout tower type building on top of a peak.

> *We stood out on a painted veranda there, too, and gasped at what lay before and around us! High white Alps below us – large crevices and rocky canyons in the earth, – and far beyond there was a hazy blueness, which almost looked like the sea – It was just "atmosphere"!!! In the few minutes we stood out there, – gasping and clicking our camera shutters. My fingers felt like they were frozen so that they'd soon drop off! … They said it was only 12 below – Centigrade (around 20 above – Fahrenheit) but it felt at least 10 F below! —*Rusty

Kit and Rusty at Jungfrau.

After dinner with Dave in Interlaken, the girls said good-bye and drove to Kandersteg to catch a 9 p.m. train. Rusty wrote that she and Kit "lost our hearts in Interlaken," and Kit wrote:

We are terribly sad to have had to leave Dave behind – the 3 of us <u>really</u> hit it off – But one of those things. We'll never see him again. I now am interested in getting a job with Esso, Shell, or etc. overseas! Missed our train at Kandersteg so are staying overnight. Train leaves at 7:15am! —Kit

The next day Rusty and Kit set off for their thirteenth country - Italy.

Italy

Italian men are fantastic! All they <u>ever</u> think about is women.

~Kit Tucker

25

Learning the Language in Italy
(November 18, 1954)

The girls spent their last month together in Italy, where the men were handsome, the letters written home slowed down, and the journal entries did, too. Rusty wrote about their arrival in Milan a month after it happened, and Kit stopped writing in her journal on December 4, though she didn't leave Italy until December 16. Kit wrote her last letter home on December 4 and sent a postcard on December 19, and Rusty wrote letters describing their Italian sojourns months after they happened.

"Our first day in Italy – and what a day! What a country! What a fabulous people!" Kit wrote from Milan on November 18, 1954. "Italian men are fantastic! All they <u>ever</u> think about is women. They notice everything. It's a riot to walk down the street – we love it – so gay, such fun."

After spending the previous night in Kandersteg, a small town in Switzerland, the girls rose early to make the 7:15 a.m. train to Brig, Switzerland.

It was pitch black when we got up and cold – Wow! 10 degrees below zero! Gulped our delicious steaming hot chocolate, stuffed down crunchy rolls and butter with apricot jam and went out into the crisp black morning with a star-studded sky. The huge black mountains loomed over us and a white half moon sat right on top of one. We drove Europa down to the station at 7 a.m. I went inside to find out where we were to put her. Door open but nobody around – I helloed, yoo-hooed and practically yodeled – no answer except a meow from an adorable, fluffy white and ginger kitten. Went back outside and sat and tooted our imperious little horn in the middle of that quiet, empty world. Finally, little old man appeared and after much directing, Europa was maneuvered onto a flat car. Dawn broke as we crunched up and down in the dry snow, waiting for the train. —Kit

Their train arrived in Brig, just before the Italian border, where the girls were supposed to change trains for the next train bound for Domodossola, Italy. "We noticed that Europa was still sitting on the track we had come in on," Kit wrote.

Much discussion in broken English, French and Italian. They were going to send her on a different train. Minutes were ticking by and in the middle of having the car papers stamped, our train pulled out – with neither Europa nor us on it! Everybody ran to the window to look – much laughing and shrugging of shoulders on the part of the officials – much frowning on the part of Rusty and Kit. Soooo – an hour later – the three of us departed on the same train. —Kit

When the train crossed the border, two Italian customs officials came on board to stamp their passports, and Kit wrote, "This was the beginning of our introduction to the Italian MAN!" and the girls were entranced.

> *Rusty and I had boned up on our phrase book and greeted them with a big smile and "Bon Giorno!" He took our passports, stamped them seriously and then flashed a big smile —- We both flipped. A dazzling white smile, olive skin, huge black eyes and a natty green uniform – who could resist? He spoke a little English so we chatted about how it was our first trip, etc., and tried out a few phrases which he got a big kick out of. His friend joined in and there was much laughing and lots of chatter, most of which nobody understood. We did gather though that they thought we were very "bella," etc. Train started up – they got off – train stopped and we sat about ten minutes. They waited outside the window – along with several other buddies – finally we started again – we waved – they waved and blew kisses! Decided we liked Italy.* —Kit

"The train began to move, and another adorable Italian customs man overheard me trying to say what time it was in Italian, and he grinned," Rusty wrote. Kit and Rusty looked up into the face of a man with "a pair of dancing, black eyes and huge dimples on either side," according to Kit.

"Very soon he was sitting with us," Rusty wrote. "And we were trying to use our few Italian words, and he was speaking his few English phrases – The train stopped in a tunnel for about 15 minutes, then backed up all the way to Brig!!"

"Our Customs friends were on the platform and when they saw the train, they came back on – chattering and exclaiming –

accompanied this time by a handsome man in civilian clothes," wrote Kit.

The girls watched as the Italian men stood around, laughing and rattling off much Italian. The important looking man pinched their cheeks, smiled, patted their hands and told them they should marry Italians. Rusty wrote:

> *They all got off and the train started to move again!!!! We were quite bewildered – and the Customs man who was sitting with us said, in labored English, — "They like you." All the way to Domodossola the three of us worked very hard at conversation – and all laughed till my sides ached!* —Rusty

The girls had traveled by train through the Simplon Tunnel, the longest continuous railway tunnel in the world. The 12.3-mile (19,823 kilometer) tunnel lies slightly northeast of the Simplon Pass and runs from Brig, Switzerland, to Iselle, Italy.

From Iselle, the train then continued through a series of tunnels for the short distance from Iselle to Domodossola, Italy, where the girls arrived on the afternoon of November 18. According to Rusty, they "alighted from the train into a strange new world!"

> *Bright, sunny, — the station was <u>swarming</u> with <u>handsome</u> men! — Many clad in a lovely shade of grayish green uniform (Customs men); — and as we walked into the Customs office to see about getting our car off the train: — <u>What</u> a <u>reception</u>!!! They swarmed around us, crying "Bella! Bella! Bella!" and speaking broken English – "Americans! – Americans!") Amid much gaiety and laughter we finally were told to return in half an hour for Europa. — We had no Italian money, we wanted to buy gas coupons, and wanted to mail some letters, so we walked from the station to streets*

with signs and names all in Italian! Such a __different__ looking language from the German and hard Swiss we had been seeing for 2 weeks! — !! And the people! No longer were they blonde blue-eyed, stocky, large-boned, and wearing drab, ill-fitted, clothing – They were now __dark__, speaking a silent language with their eyes, either dressed well or poorly, but with a style and an intriguing flair – Lots of black – Lots of color! And Kit and I decided anything must be an excuse to wear a uniform! Never saw so many different ones!! Every color, every style, — every kind of varied "head dress" … all looking terribly official – and terribly good-looking! —Rusty

Drawing by Rusty of Europa loaded on the railroad car.

When Kit and Rusty returned to the train station, they encountered the most handsome man they had ever seen, according to both a letter from Rusty and a page in Kit's journal. Wearing a green uniform, he escorted them to Europa's railroad car.

[He] couldn't speak a word of English – so we walked __and__ walked and walked, not speaking but smiling and nodding – Kit and I were fighting back the giggles when we __finally__ arrived to find Europa, still __loaded__, and sitting far down at the end of several empty cars! A little man scurried around and put boards between the cars, and then I had to back it off!!!!! Whew! Then the Customs man said "sugareetes?" "liquor?" – And proceeded to open the back door. I thought he was going to check, — perhaps he didn't believe that we didn't have any, but instead he crawled in on top of our luggage!

(And even minus Kit's one big suitcase, the back seat was <u>loaded high!!</u>) —Rusty

Kit wrote, "We thought he wanted to check thru our baggage so we opened the door. Things came tumbling out – a peanut can – pair of shoes – book! We blushed."

It turned out the handsome man wanted a ride.

The young man poked his head and shoulders in and we thought "Oh! Dear! He's going to take everything out – but then his legs and feet disappeared too! Looked in and there he was wrapped around our luggage lying down - sort of - on top of it, looking breathless but pleased – waiting for us to drive him back to the station! Off we scooted with him gasping and gurgling away to himself in Italian and us laughing hysterically! —Kit

Rusty wrote, "His knees were almost touching the ceiling and his head was between ours in the front – so funny!! Then back at the station he unfolded himself from the back seat and motioned that I was to go with him."

"He emerged slightly ruffled (but still fabulously handsome!) and murmuring, 'Mama, mia!' – but – otherwise completely unperturbed." Kit added.

While Kit remained in the car, Rusty walked back to the Customs office where the Italian men refused to give her back her Carnet.

Couldn't imagine why and I was getting worried, when I realized they only wanted me to remain in Domodossola that night. They disapproved of our going on to Milan – and told me of all the fun we could have that evening – going dancing, – eating pizza – etc. – <u>So</u> cute!! —Rusty

Kit found herself the center of attention outside. "People came over and stared at me and made various comments or argued among themselves as to whether I was French (because of the license) or English or American." When she told them she was American, "They laughed, said, 'Bella, signora,' and walked off still arguing and looking back at the car."

After about 15 minutes, Rusty returned and "practically the entire Customs Office was with her." After escorting Rusty to the car, the men shook their hands, and waved as the girls drove away. "What a wonderful reception it was to Italy!!!!" Rusty wrote.

> *From Domodossola we drove through mountains – very Italian mountains – covered with vineyards, Spanish style homes – pink and yellow and white; – along beautiful lakes, summer resort towns and beaches, – Kit saw her very first palm trees! – The roof was open in Europa, the sun poured in, warm and friendly – and we said "We have arrived." —Rusty*

26

Sightseeing in Milan
(November 18 – November 19, 1954)

"Milan is a <u>big</u> city!!! And the Italians are crazier drivers than the French! – But we made it somehow," Rusty wrote her mother from Rome a month later. After a relatively short drive, about 113 kilometers according to today's roads, the girls arrived in Milan and began the search for a place to stay. Rusty wrote, "Searched and searched for an inexpensive hotel – but they simply are not to be found! The <u>cheapest</u> there cost <u>3,000 lire</u>, which is $4.80 – ridiculous!"

While in Milan, the girls did some sightseeing and toured several places, including the Duomo, La Scala (Teatro alla Scala), and the church of Santa Maria della Grazie. Rusty wrote:

The next morning we went to the <u>Duomo</u>. [A] vast gothic cathedral, completely constructed in <u>white</u> <u>marble</u> – <u>Covered</u> with delicate pinnacles and <u>hundreds</u> of statues; — is 355 ft. high, and its spire *has a gold statue of the Madonna, — reflects like a golden <u>beacon</u> in the sunlight. — Inside, it is dark, formal, <u>plain</u>, — but the windows were <u>BEAUTIFUL</u> again! Really European cathedrals have the most brilliant, deep, richly-colored windows you can possibly imagine! You can't help but <u>gasp</u> when you first see them!* —Rusty

The girls passed by La Scala, "the most famous opera house in the world," but were soon disappointed. Although they were in what Rusty called, "the very <u>home</u> and birthplace of <u>opera</u>," the girls wouldn't be able to see a performance. The opera season wouldn't begin until early December.

Next — we went to the convent of the Church of Santa Maria della Grazie — entered a door, paid for a ticket, walked thru a small gate and into a second large door, turned, — and there, at the far end of the room was The Last Supper! Certainly never expected it, but the painting thrilled me <u>more</u> than any other work of art I had seen thus far — Another amazing thing: during the war, the other <u>three</u> <u>walls</u> of the Convent were completely <u>destroyed</u>, and only the wall on which the Last Supper is painted, was left standing. <u>A true miracle</u>. ... It faded terrifically from being exposed to sun and rain for so long but it is still one of the most beautiful paintings I have ever ever seen! They have reconstructed the long room but have left the other three walls and the ceiling completely plain and white; and the Last Supper has such perspective, that as you enter the room you feel drawn toward it, and as if you could continue walking – right into the Last Supper – We stood in awe and respect for a long time. —Rusty

The girls stopped at a gas station to ask directions for the drive to Venice. "By the time we were finished we had eight students around too trying to help – all shouting and arguing – terribly funny!" Kit wrote.

The girls were astonished, delighted, and exhilarated by the fervid attentions of the Italian young men. Still more surprising were some unanticipated styles of toilets! Kit wrote about both in her letter home on November 18. About the men, she wrote:

> *Their main pastime is adoring women. You can't walk down the street without having every 9 out of 10 men smile broadly and tell you how beautiful you are or sort of hiss thru their tooth (Italian equivalent of the wolf whistle – I think). They are completely disarming about it though and we are getting a huge charge out of it. Great morale builder. You don't dare let it show that you notice the comments though – otherwise, they are encouraged. You can't even look at them - this is a sign of interest and means they can proceed further. It is all completely wild and crazy —- and wonderful! We love it! Never saw so many handsome and dashing looking men in just a few hours as we did to-day! I may come back married to an Italian count after all!* —Kit

About her first encounter with a "squat" toilet, Kit wrote:

> *Say – ran into my first real continental type john today – I missed them in France but Rusty found a couple – and found it, of all places, Bud – in a brand new shiny Shell Station!!! We've gotten eagle-eyed about ferreting out "Toilette" signs as we whiz along the highway so we saw this one to-day – pulled in and got some gas. I asked for their key – went into beautifully appointed anteroom with sink – towels, soap. Everything lovely enamel and tile. Opened the inside door – stepped in – almost went thru the floor – literally! (Hope you aren't shocked – I'm getting terribly basic!). All there was – was a large porcelain square in the floor (albeit very new and*

shiny) with a hole in the middle and two oblong pieces on either side for your feet! I just about died! Stood there leaning against the door laughing all by myself. —Kit

Punting in Verona and Venice
(November 19 – November 22, 1954)

The girls left Milan late in the afternoon and drove along "very crowded highways" to Verona, the home of Romeo and Juliet in Shakespeare's play. After finding a room in a hotel, Rusty and Kit ate their first Italian spaghetti. In the morning, the girls walked to Piazza Bra, the largest piazza in Verona.

In the piazza, the girls discovered a huge Roman amphitheater, Verona Arena or Arena di Verona, built sometime around 30 A.D. The third largest amphitheater in the world, it once seated over 20,000 spectators. Had it been summer, the girls might have been among the thousands to see a festival event, such as the opera *Aida*.

Rusty said the amphitheater was in almost perfect condition and called it a "huge hulk of timelessness in the midst of a bustling little city dressed in modern clothes, and doing modern things – The contrast between the people who walk <u>on</u> the streets, and the streets themselves is completely fantastic!!"

As Kit and Rusty wandered around Verona looking for Juliet's balcony, they found themselves in the middle of a market place. Rusty wrote:

> *We have seen open-air markets all over Europe, but <u>none</u> can compare with those of Italy! <u>Literally</u> everything from soup to nuts and more!!! And the people who are selling! Fat dark women; fat, moustached men, and handsome young fish-mongers – Fabulous! Bartering and haggling over the prices – in rapid-fire Italian –*
>
> *We noticed, too, that all the old men on the street (walking or riding bicycles) wore black heavy woolen capes … and they had one side draped up over the other shoulder – So even the old men look terribly dashing!!! And all the older women wore heavy black woolen shawls with fringe one or two feet long – draped and wrapped round them – Both Kit and I wanted a shawl <u>and</u> a cape!!*
> —Rusty

They never did find the balcony, but Kit wrote that the market was "marvelous" and added in her journal that they "had [a] delicious puffy thing called fritello – light as a feather donut without a hole in it type."

"After bidding farewell to Romeo and Juliet in Verona," Rusty wrote, the girls "zoomed" on the *Autostrada* toward Venice. The highway was flat and wide and "blossoming" with road-side advertisement. Rusty wrote that Italy is the only country in Europe that equals the United States for billboards. "Other countries don't even have a <u>tiny</u> sign!" They knew they were near Venice when "masses of gasoline stations were clustered about …

every kind of gasoline in Europe including Shell and Esso (our standbys)."

The girls parked Europa in a huge garage structure and walked toward the canal where they found water taxis, instead of buses, going to different sections of Venice. "We bought our tickets and waited on the floating and rocking dock, sitting on benches, and being very cold and very excited," Rusty wrote. When the water taxi finally came, the girls clambered aboard. Rusty described the boats as "long" with "many seats – some outside and some inside."

With their stop written down on a piece of paper, the girls "showed it to the little man who helped everyone step over the gangplank."

> *We scampered off ... and My Heavens! We were in Venice! The sun was just setting, and over the water and the view of Venice across the lagoon was unbelievable ... right away we knew we were in a fairyland ... this couldn't be real!* —Rusty

Because Italy was so expensive and since their car was parked in a garage, the girls decided to stay at a youth hostel to save money. Rusty wrote:

> *We started down the narrow walk along the water, boats tied up to wooden pegs, men unloading fish, little stores with their fruits and vegetables and fish hanging in the windows, tiny little "alleys" going down between the buildings; young boys looked at us and shouted "Americans"! "Hostel!" And by their cries we were directed across two bridges and finally down a narrow "passageway" just wide enough for one person ... past open doors, smells of fish and bread, little children running and shouting and*

playing, on and on until we came to a very small kind of courtyard.
... Two young Italian girls responded to our insistent knocking, and
though they could speak no English, we finally understood that the
Hostel was closed until 6:00, and we couldn't get in until then. We
were freezing, the Hostel was stony and cold, and our arms were
aching from the suitcases, so we finally induced them to keep our
suitcases, and we said we would return at 6:00. —Rusty

At 4:00 p.m., after leaving their luggage at the hostel, the girls
boarded a *motoscafo* (water bus) and headed across the lagoon to
Venice "proper" – and to St. Mark's Square. Rusty described the
sights:

... graceful black gondolas gliding everywhere, all shapes of boats
winding their ways through the canals, the beautiful Palace of
Doges, the beautiful dome of the Basilica of St. Mark, — all bathed
in rosy golden light ... the rippling peaceful waters reflecting the
sunset that covered the entire sky with lavender and blue and pink
and peach and gold and deep rose. ... We were in a land of dreams.
... St. Mark's Square was filled with people, adorable children
feeding the myriads of pigeons fluttering around, handsome men,
and happy clusters of families. ... The tourist office sent us to a hotel
(we decided the cold-out-of-the-way Hostel was not for us in
Venice!), and we walked right under the clock (famous Clock Tower
which tells the hours and the daily position of the sun and moon;
and the two statues strike a gigantic bell every quarter and half hour
and hour), — around a little corner to our hotel – Had a nice big
room, but freezing! —Rusty

As they walked around Venice, "About 2 million men tried to
pick us up," according to Kit. The girls politely declined, went
back to the Hostel and retrieved their bags "without anyone

knowing." After they picked up their suitcases, Rusty wrote, "[We] stood on the deck of the little motorboat as we slipped through the black water, with stars, twinkling lights of the islands reflecting in the soft waves ... mmmmmmmmmm ... mmmm ...."

Gondola in a funeral procession in Venice.

"We had dinner in our hotel and went to bed early. It was so cold in our room that we wore socks, and two sweaters to bed, and our hands were so cold we couldn't even write a page in our diary," Rusty wrote. The girls later discovered that the cold they were experiencing in Venice was part of an unusually extreme cold spell throughout Italy.

The following morning, on Sunday, November 21, Kit and Rusty awoke warm and cozy in bed before dressing quickly and rushing downstairs for hot chocolate and buns. Bundled up (Rusty wore a sweater and jacket and coat and two pairs of socks), they ambled about Venice, exploring and taking pictures. Rusty wrote:

*Imagine icy water lapping up under frigid stone, and your poor
little feet on top of that … brrr … but we were so in love with
Venice that we could have frozen to death, and we wouldn't have
cared. People were strolling everywhere and everything was so
bright and gay!* —Rusty

Rusty continued her description of Venice in a letter to her
mother in South Dakota:

*Canals wind through Venice, cutting her into one gigantic jigsaw
puzzle … and of course the "streets" are only wide enough for one
person … or two slim people to pass each other at the most … and
the bldgs. go straight up from the "streets" and from the canals.
Such a funny sensation to walk around, Kit and I wound round and
round, away from the Main Canal and the Lagoon, into the back
canals and streets, over tiny, tiny bridges, into dirty little
courtyards, watched little boys pulling a gondola along a narrow
canal and playing in empty gondolas which were tied up to the front
doors; wandered through the fish market, stopped to watch and
listen to the women arguing about the fish – their tongues bubbling
over this "round" language, their hands gesticulating wildly, — an
apron tied around their abundant waists, black dresses, black
shawls, black and graying hair pulled to huge thick buns, their skin
brown and smooth, — carrying groaning straw baskets bulging
with unwrapped fish, tomatoes, oranges, and green spinach, brown
paper parcels of macaroni and spaghetti, — and hearing voices
crying "Signorina, Signorina?"* —Rusty

After coffee and lunch in a little café overlooking the Venice
Lagoon, the girls assembled in front of the Compagnia Italiana
Turismo (C.I.T., a tourist office) and joined a guided group of 10

for a ride in gondolas. Rusty wrote, "As I saw the gondolas coming toward us, I felt I was in a fairy book tale."

Kit and Rusty slipped "gracefully" into a black, long, and sleek gondola. In the boat, they joined two other tourists, a man from China and a man from Columbia, and the handsomest gondolier (according to Rusty). She wrote, "I fell in love with him immediately, but Kit fell for the gondolier of the other gondola in our party ... and so they 'made eyes' at each other across the canals, but all I had to do was to look up ... (ha!)."

> *The movement of the gondoliers is indescribable: graceful, elegant, rippling, perfect balance and rhythm. ... We slipped through the gentle waters, past the once-elegant mansions with their "barber poles" out in front (for tying their gondolas to), past the home of Robert Browning, where he lived and died alone, past lacy Venetian architecture, under wide arching bridges, stopping to visit two churches. —Rusty*

They eased into narrow back canals, dark and hidden, according to Rusty, gliding so close to people's homes, they could reach out and touch their front doors. They glided past the Doge's Palace (Palazzo Ducale) and the Bridge of Sighs (Ponte dei Sospiri) and then out again into the lagoon. Rusty wrote, "Just as the sun was setting, making the entire world rosy and golden – the colors of the sky rippling in the water. ... I felt like a child and wanted to say "I don't want to get out, let's go 'round again!"

After saying good-bye to the gondolier and guide, the man from Columbia invited the girls for a cappuccino. "And over our frothy coffee we learned that he is the aide to the ambassador to Holland," Rusty wrote. "He was on vacation, and complained about the frigidness and somberness of the Dutch people … he said he came to Italy for sun and to dance and to laugh."

The Columbian and the gondolier were just a couple of several men the girls encountered during their one full day in Venice. Rusty wrote:

> *Kit and I are completely convinced that from the age of two they think of nothing else but women! The fathers must take their young sons out and lecture to them about the opposite sex that passes by! I was standing in St. Marco's Square, and suddenly a handsome man appeared at my elbow and while I aimed and took a picture of the Clock, he sang opera to me! I moved back near Kit to take another picture, and he followed, singing opera to me all the while. He must have followed me about, never saying anything but just singing, for about 15 minutes and then he wistfully wandered off.* —Rusty

She wrote about the 10 young gondoliers trooping along behind, chattering and singing gaily, "Bella! Bella! Bella!" and the Navy captain who spoke English. The only way they could get rid of him after he walked with them for half an hour was to take his address and promise to write and say where they would be in Rome.

Kit wrote in her journal, "Told lies. Finally convinced him!" After cappuccino with the Columbian man and dinner with a "lively Italian boy," the girls returned to the hotel. Kit wrote, "Just as we got to the desk, 8 Italian sailors walked by." The girls made a lunge for the door. "As I turned around at the head of the stairs they were pointing through the door. The desk man was pushing them back – we ran!"

In spite of all the attention (or perhaps because of it), the girls loved Italian men. Rusty wrote her mother, "They are so cute, so unoffensive, so terribly naive in their unnaivete."

The next morning, the girls hurriedly shopped and discovered a "fabulous store" where Kit bought a tan leather bag for $3. She wrote that the leather, Venetian lace, and glassware were "unequaled anywhere!" The girls climbed upon a *motoscafo* and hung over the edge, "as we waved goodbye to Venice, promising to return."

28

Shopping in Florence
(November 22 – November 24, 1954)

It was almost noon on November 22 when the girls left Venice. After they retrieved Europa from the garage, the girls filled up the car with gas. The attendants were "wonderful" and "lots of fun." The girls then headed south to Florence.

> *We really zoomed and the road was wide and smooth, and then …*
> *the flat plains of Italy began to bulge … and soon we were twisting*
> *back and forth, as the hills loomed larger and larger. … Hills that*
> *were rusty and chocolatey and covered with cactus and small green*
> *shrubs, rocky, - we climbed and climbed, never-ending hair-pin*
> *curves; back and forth, back and forth, until we got the giggles, and*
> *my arm ached from turning the steering wheel so much! The day*
> *was graying, and the valleys took on a purple glow … huge*
> *abandoned mansions perched magnificently on a lone hill-top, little*
> *adobe huts nestled in a draw, chickens ran cackling by the road, old*
> *bent men herded romping sheep among the rocks, - the country was*
> *a wild, rough, country – a poor one – and it was Italy!*

It grew colder and the wind began to blow ... we stopped at a wayside inn to have some hot coffee. ... It was large and empty, and a round little woman brought us hot milk and coffee and sweet bread. ... She spoke no English but wanted to talk with us ... and finally she brought out a large folder of pictures, newspaper clippings, etc., and showed us a Christmas card she had received from Tyrone Power and Linda Christian. This little back inn had been a favorite "hiding-place" for Tyrone, and they stopped here on their honeymoon, after being married in Rome. There were many snapshots of them all together, and there was a long newspaper article and large picture of when the Powers visited this woman's daughter who is living in the States now. She married an American soldier shortly after the War. This woman was so proud and so excited and is sooo fond of Americans! It was hard to get away from her ... but we must hurry, — the day was growing darker and the curving road was dangerous ... there were many sheer drops a long way down! —Rusty

It was dark and about 5:45 p.m. when the girls entered Florence, stopping every block to ask directions to American Express. They arrived just 10 minutes before it closed but in time to receive "letters galore." The girls were jubilant.

The people at American Express recommended a hotel just across the street, so the girls checked in to the hotel, and, just as they began reading their mail, remembered they'd left the car parked on the street. Kit wrote in her journal, "Ran madly out – yup, it happened again! Window torn open. Light on. Rusty's overnight case gone – my darling little [Agfa] camera – just sick. This is tougher than the last – All those pictures of Dave, Jungfrau and Venice – can't <u>stand it!</u>"

So upset she didn't want to tell her mother, Rusty wrote, "Later that night we had spaghetti, made friends with the waiters and went to bed."

But Rusty was forced to tell the story to her mother five months after the incident when the local insurance agent in South Dakota told Alice about the robbery. Furious with the insurance agent, only then, in April 1955, did Rusty describe what happened.

> *Kit and I were rushing, and we were terribly anxious to hear from home! And also I was supposed to have my pictures (the ones I sent you) there. Well, we didn't rush because of that but we thought of it all the way, and as we neared Florence, we realized if we did hurry, we could be there before it closed at 6:00. ... And we arrived in front of American Express just at ten minutes to 6:00. ... It was a busy street, in front of the river, I parked immediately in front of Am. Ex.; and there was a policeman on the corner (one door away!) directing traffic; it was still a little light; and because to get your mail you must go in person with your passport, we both went in. Kit received some money from home and that took a long time to get cashed; I received many letters ... and we were both sooo happy! Am. Ex. recommended a hotel just across the street. We ran over there, taking special notice of the policeman and of the car — everything okay. ... We dashed in, got a room (didn't look at it or anything) ... asked where there was a garage and dashed out to drive to the garage. ...*

> *The light was on, one window (the same one) had been pried open again ... my little suitcase (they probably thought it contained jewels) and Kit's new German camera were gone. ... This hit three times as hard as before; and just after we had been so happily receiving mail from you. ... We went immediately to the police ...*

and were there 2 hours – the Italian policemen are the most stupid things I have ever met in my life. … Nothing disturbs them – they don't care!!!! I was completely sick for one week. … I couldn't write. … I couldn't think. … Florence was completely ruined for me … and I have only very bad memories and impressions of it … that is one reason I want to return … because I know it really is a beautiful city. —Rusty

On Tuesday, November 23, depressed from the most recent robbery, the girls did some shopping in Florence "[Florence is] the most fabulous place to shop in the World!" Rusty said in a letter written the day after the theft. The girls spent the entire day on the Ponte Vecchio, where shops selling jewelry, leather, cameo, and lace are scattered along a covered bridge which crosses over the Arno River. "Shopped like mad and got some wonderful things," Kit wrote in her journal. Rusty wrote:

The bridge is very old and very famous, and was the only bridge that the Germans didn't blow up! (Ponte means bridge, and Vecchio means old). We had intended to do some sight-seeing that afternoon, but we got completely carried away, and the entire day – until 7:30 – was spent wishing and wanting and buying a few gifts! —Rusty

Kit added, "Loads of fun – very cheering up."

Tired from shopping, the girls ate a luscious dinner and flirted with the cute waiters at the same little trattoria where they had eaten the night before. Rusty wrote, "We pulled out our Italian phrase book and they had so much fun looking at it! We were the last ones to leave, and then we went 'home' to bed."

At 9 a.m., the girls climbed aboard a bus for their first guided tour of a European city. On the tour, they visited the two Medici Chapels at the Basilica of San Lorenzo. Rusty wrote:

> *The Medici family was the greatest patron of the Arts that has ever existed, I believe; in Italy as elsewhere … their name is everywhere in Italy. Florence, in 1422, elected Giovanni Bicci dei Medici (Medici means "medicines") and the important male members of the Medici family were doctors. Some of the females married various Kings throughout Europe; including one of the Kings of England – can't remember which one now -). Until the year 1737 the Medici name governed the city, and gave it a host of churches and palaces, and added to and beautified villas and the streets of the city.*
> *—Rusty*

Rusty was particularly impressed with the New Sacristy, one of the chapels designed by Michelangelo. It was intended as a mausoleum for the Medicis but was never finished. Rusty wrote of the reclining, sculpted figures representing four times of day:

> *[…] there are two beautiful statues: a man representing "Dawn" and a woman representing "Dusk"; and on the other side are two others: "Day" (man) and "Night" (woman). And you can only see them to really be awed by their strength and perfect graceful beauty. Strange, though, don't you think, that woman is Dusk and Night – I would have thought the other way around. … Of all the statues "Night" is the most beautiful and most admired. It was done by Michelangelo after the fall of the republic in 1530, and the poet [Giovanni] Strozzi wrote this poem about it: "The night you see sleeping so sweetly was sculptured by an angel in this stone; and although sleeping, has life —- wake her, if you don't believe, she will speak to you." But Michelangelo responded with, "Thankful I am*

for sleep and to be of stone, whilst disaster and shame are lasting,
not to see and not to feel is my great luck; so let me sleep and do not
raise your voice." —Rusty

Next on their tour, the girls visited the octagonal Battistero di San Giovanni, one of the oldest buildings in Florence, built in the 11th century. According to Rusty:

> *It is very famous because of its three doors in gilded bronze – all*
> *extremely interesting and beautiful. The most important is the*
> *Paradise Door (named that because Michelangelo, admiring*
> *enthusiastically the marvelous work of art, declared it worthy to*
> *close the gate of Paradise), [which] is the masterpiece of Lorenzo*
> *Ghiberti who worked on it for 17 years! It was finished in 1424. The*
> *door is divided into 10 tablets, each one representing scenes from the*
> *Old Testament; and you could spend an hour or more studying all*
> *the minute details and beauty of sculpturing that is there. The*
> *inside is all marble and adorned with mosaics.* —Rusty

The tour continued with a stop at the Cathedral of Santa Maria del Fiore, where two American boys, John Stokes and Dick "Dusty" Rhodes, began following Kit and Rusty around. Also known as Duomo, the cathedral was begun in 1296 and completed in 1436. According to Rusty, "The cathedral and the bell tower are both colored in a delicate shade of pink and white marble … and they look like birthday cakes."

> *Then we drove high up above the city along a gorgeous drive – on*
> *the Piazzale Michelangelo … only of course the clouds were low and*
> *gray and the fog was thick. … Tall stately cypress and white statues*
> *dotted the gardens and the city … and the Arno River wound*
> *gracefully along the side of round domes and tall towers. …*
> *Churches everywhere!* —Rusty

At the Palazzo Pitti, Rusty and Kit recognized several paintings. "I saw sooo many paintings I knew so well!" Rusty wrote to her mother, "including, among many many many, the Madonna of the [Chair] by Raphael. ... To really go into all the things we saw in Florence would involve me writing a guide book, and I would much rather give you impressions of other things, not written in books – and you?"

After the tour, Kit and Rusty had lunch with three girls whom they had met on the top of Jungfrau (and who were on the tour as well) and the two American boys. The girls soon discovered that John was also from South Dakota and Dusty was going back to America on the RMS *Mauretania*, the same ship Kit would be taking. "Kit and I felt quite proud when we had to read the menu and order for everyone —- And to think how little Italian I knew then compared to what I know now. ... he he. ... "

After an afternoon spent doing a little more "exploring" of shops, and of standing completely speechless and awestruck at the sight of Michelangelo's statue of David. ... (one of the most beautiful statues I've ever seen. We stood and gazed for half an hour, and I could have remained another hour; —), we fell exhausted on our beds in the hotel, and decided to go to bed early, when the two Americans phoned and suggested they take us out to dinner – needless to say, we jumped at that idea! We ate in a lovely place with guitars and violins and accordian and a singer ... who looked just like a gypsy, and sang Spanish and Italian gypsy songs ... terribly exciting! And then John drove Dusty and Kit and me all around Florence in his brand new Studebaker – the real streamlined one! —Rusty

29

Feasting in Italy
(November 25, 1954)

It was Thanksgiving Day, and the girls were planning to drive all the way to Rome, but after a late night with John and Dusty, the two got a late start.

> *Dead – slept until 10:00 am. Had breakfast ... Over to American Express – natch – John and Dusty there – very funny we had all just gotten up – wanted us to lunch – said no had to drive on – maybe we'll see Dusty in Sorrento or Rome.* —Kit

After breakfast, the girls packed up Europa and "drove out in an Italian drizzle, leaving Florence behind."

> *Drove over the windingest, twistingist, sharpest-cornered road I've ever seen! – Never knew that Italy was so hilly! There are huge mountainous hills, and large crevices, and actual cliffs, — The terrain actually is more mountainous than hilly, only the ground is kind of clay-like. – and the landscape kept changing ... from groves*

upon groves of <u>olive</u> <u>trees</u> <u>covering</u> the hillsides, and lovely yellow and pink "stucco" villas perched high on the tops of hills overlooking tree-covered valleys, — Needle-like cypress trees, graceful and lovely, lined the highways and private driveways ... and appeared as exclamation points against the far horizons —- to a land that was almost desert-like barren, mild, — only scrubby brush and tufts of long grass growing on the hills – And the towns we drove through – surrounded by high stone walls, and each having a large dome-covered gate through which you must pass. ... Most of them seemed to be deserted except for a few chickens here and there. ... We "whooped for joy" when we saw a big <u>turkey</u>!! —Rusty

Just as they entered Viterbo, a town in the Lazio region of central Italy, Europa's right back tire went flat. Rusty wrote, "I hiked on up the road and a very nice man in a Garage who spoke only Italian came and changed our tire for us. – But he couldn't fix it till tomorrow so we don't know yet what caused it. – We didn't like this part of Thanksgiving at all!!"

The girls found a "very nice little hotel" around the corner from the garage, and at 8 p.m. found a restaurant to eat their Thanksgiving dinner. Rusty wrote:

[We] couldn't find tacchino (turkey) or pollo (chicken) anywhere, — so this was our turkey and cranberries and pumpkin pie:
1st course - Macaroni with tomato sauce and butter and cheese (Macaroni was like <u>long</u> flat noodles)
2nd - Rolli de Veal (rolled around a very spicy and very good dressing and then sliced) and spinach
3rd - Cappucino (<u>terribly</u> <u>strong</u> black coffee served with <u>whipped</u> <u>milk</u> – good!)

And that was it. Wish I were home for today. —Rusty

30

Celebrity Gazing in Rome
(November 26, 1954)

With their newly mended tire, the girls left Viterbo and began the journey on the winding road to Rome. "Woopee!" Kit wrote in her journal. "Warmer weather!" The landscape changed. Kit thought the countryside looked strange with its "olive trees, cypress trees, bare land, caves all along the road with people living in them and tabac shops in them!"

"It got very exciting," wrote Rusty. "We kept saying 'Rome' over and over ... was it really possible??? Were we really going to be in Rome??"

> Kit was very clever with the map and we came in on a highway which led us straight into the heart of the city and into Piazza di Spagna, American Express being our object, of course. We saw Amexco (Am-Ex-Co) just ahead of us, less than a block away, and suddenly we were forced to turn right onto a one-way street ... no

place to park and we had to keep going and going and going and going. … We were almost frantic, afraid we were going to be hopelessly lost … finally we could turn left then we had to go blocks and blocks and blocks again before we could make another left, and of course by this time we were far far far from Piazza di Spagna and pretty well confused. … With the help of a policeman we found a garage in which to put the car, and then walked about 5 blocks to Amexco. —Rusty

After collecting their mail, the girls asked for directions to the Post Office, bought a map and an Italian dictionary, and started out.

Rusty at the Trevi Fountain.

We wound down tiny cobblestone streets crowded with women selling fruit from their little carts, boys carrying heavy boxes of meat, vegetables, etc., on their heads, men standing in the warm hazy sunlight,

Kit at the Trevi Fountain

… and suddenly the streets opened up into a small square, and there was the Trevi Fountain! Quite well enclosed by bldgs., but how enormous! Many people were there, and we excitedly skipped over to the edge, and whipped out our camera, and then I looked down and who should be standing by the fountain taking a picture of some red-headed man, but Jane Powell! Our first day in Rome and we see an American movie star! So I took 2 or 3 pictures of the fountain and of Jane! And then we walked down beside her and took pictures of each other. Jane and her man-friend

left arm-in-arm and we were sure we would hear of Jane's sudden elopement to Rome, or something ... but we didn't. Kit and I both threw our coins in! And then mapped our way to the Post Office. —Rusty

With little understanding of the Italian language, Rusty vainly attempted to mail a package back to the U.S. "And oh my, what a struggle thence ensued!" As a little man fired away in Italian, she tried to set a value on the package, to insure it, and tell him that it must go through Customs. "Impossible!"

Hearing the commotion, an American girl came running over and asked if Rusty and Kit needed help. Rusty wrote:

> *We pounced on her "yes"! And she dashed over to another line of people and brought back two young men. ... Who turned out to be Alberto and Rekin! Alberto nobly translated and handled the entire transaction. (Ignorant of the whole procedure I was quite concerned until I heard from Carla saying they had received the package.) The girl was Sylvia, (chubby, very arty, and what a Brooklyn accent!) and she told us to come to Taverna Margutta when we returned to Rome because they all ate there every noon and evening, and the "restaurant" was very inexpensive, the hangout for all the artists of Rome (known and unknown), and there was a guitarist, etc. ... We said we would, thanked them profusely, and said goodbye. ... Little did we know that we would later become such good friends!*
> —Rusty

After a light lunch of soup and salad and tea in a little English style "tea room," the girls found Europa and began winding their way "through this ancient, unique, and intriguing city." Kit wrote in her journal:

[…] we were looking lost and an Italian fellow knocked on the window and asked if we needed help – we did, so he did – very well too – runs a tie shop nearby where we were and his cousin is a big tenor with La Scala. Gave us his card – Fast workers these Italians.
—Kit

With plans to return to Rome in a few days, the girls began the drive on to Naples.

But it grew dark terribly fast, and we wanted to see Naples in the daytime, so we stopped soon in <u>Formia</u> … dark, so we couldn't see really what it looked like … found a nice hotel, fairly inexpensive (for Italy, that is), put Europa in a garage, and ate spaghetti for dinner; had one of those delicious <u>rare</u> baths, and flopped into bed.
—Rusty

ENGLISH	ITALIAN	PRONOUNCED:
MILAN	MILANO	Mee LÁNO
ITALY	ITALIA	EeTÁLYA
PADOVA	PADOVA	PÁDUA
VENICE	VENEZIA	VENÁTSYA
FLORENCE	FIRENZE	FEERÉNZAY
ROME	ROMA	RÓMA
NAPLES	NAPOLI	NÁPOLEE
CAPRI	CAPRI	CÁPRI
GENOA	GENOA	GÉNOA

Excerpt from a letter home where Rusty explains Italian pronounciation.

31

Sunning on the Amalfi Coast
(November 27 – December 2, 1954)

When Rusty awoke the next morning, she was surprised by what she saw through the window of their hotel room.

I got up first, went into our bathroom (about the 2nd time we had a bathroom all of our own!), and pushed open the shutters to let in some light, — my eyes popped open like saucers! There on my right was blue blue blue sea! The Mediterranean! And below me were palm trees, white plaster bldgs., children playing in brilliant sunshine, women leaning out of windows – their plump arms gesticulating expressively to their excited Italian words. … After I caught my breath, I rushed into our bedroom, pushed open the enormous shutters on our two windows, opened the glass double doors, … and told Kit to "Open your eyes, and gaze on Paradise!" She did, and there before her lay a white sandy bay and this wide expanse of azure blue sea. … Sun streamed in. … And I don't know when there have been two more excited girls! We jumped to the balcony and ohhed and ahhed and took pictures ... couldn't wait to get started. ... Had hot chocolate and buns beside wide sunny windows overlooking that same blue blue ... and watched children playing around two palm trees. ... With Europa's roof wide open, we sang our way toward Napoli! —Rusty

Looking out their hotel window - first view of the Mediterranean.

Rusty wrote more about their trip to Naples and Pompeii:

We were driving in the warm sun, and in a very short time we were entering Naples ... the most fantastic city I've ever seen!! Well ... almost ... A white, yellow, pink, and orange city, with everything being terribly sunny and warm and gay and that beautiful blue bay; but noisy! There were clothes hanging out to dry everywhere! On the sidewalks along the main highway throughout the city! People, walking along the street shopping, had to duck under shirts and trousers and sheets and underwear that had been strung on rope between poles treacherously stuck into cracks in the sidewalk before the apartments... I thought I was seeing things, really! —Rusty

After buying gas and asking the way to Pompeii, the girls decided they didn't want to take the *Autostrada* to Pompeii. "We didn't want to miss a thing!" Rusty wrote.

> *We took the other road which led down near the bay in Naples. ...*
> *Well! We didn't miss anything all right! Unbelievable here, too. ...*
> *The streets completely covered and littered with "things" ... people*
> *... everywhere;-dirty, naked children yelling, running, playing in*
> *the streets, old men and women, thin and fat, dark and wrinkled.*
> *Sitting on chairs in the middle of the sidewalks, sunning*
> *themselves; young boys peddling bicycles in the street, singing gaily*
> *and heartily; and the horses and wagons! I believe every means of*
> *transporting food, wine, clothing, furniture, etc. includes the horse*
> *and wagon! What a sight it was to see old men, swarthy wrinkled*
> *skin, with thick white moustaches; and young men – dark, virile and*
> *handsome, sitting astride a wagon full of tomatoes or oranges,*
> *lemons and apples, or all kinds of greens; or five-gallon jugs of wine*
> *– green glass swathed in woven straw ... behind beautiful high-*
> *spirited horses (that anyone could have won a prize with in a horse*
> *show!) ... pulling these loads ... and so gaily decorated with silver*
> *and ribbons and bright-colored pompoms! And everyone singing the*
> *sentimental Neapolitan love songs – that floated through the air*
> *above the cries of the children and the fruit callers.* —Rusty

For two hours, the girls drove on narrow streets with horses and children. Rusty wrote:

> *[...] then some children began throwing things at me. ... How out*
> *of place I felt, and how terribly such a foreigner! We should have*
> *had an American flag flying somewhere then; later we discovered*
> *that Italians are not so very fond of the French, and I guess our*
> *French license plate wasn't the most diplomatic thing we could have*

been displaying. ... Anyway, it was terribly interesting, and I was also very glad when we got out of the city ... we drove along the bay for a short way, then out over, through one Italian village after the other, and very shortly we arrived at Pompeii!! —Rusty

"Even Richard Halliburton didn't do it justice!" Rusty wrote about Pompeii, referring to her childhood book, *Richard Halliburton's Complete Book of Marvels.*

One of the most fascinating places we had been on the entire trip! Our imaginations carried us vividly and rapidly back two thousand years ago. ... What a civilization they had! How very refined and wise and intelligent they were ... except when they entered their "colosseums" – ha. —Rusty

After paying 60 cents to enter Pompeii (expensive at the time), the girls decided they needed a guide and paid an extra $2 for one.

But it was worth it! You can't see Pompeii without a guide; and the one we had was just perfect! There were just the 3 of us; and he was so friendly, and was so anxious to show us everything and he philosophized and told us stories and really was just fabulous! —Rusty

Rusty wrote about how well preserved Pompeii was. She described the bright colored political signs on the walls which asked people to please vote for a candidate. "But as the guide said, they were worded so kindly, praying to the people to please have the kindness to think of them and vote for them."

Rusty was impressed with the decorations in the houses, painted on the walls, still brightly visible.

And as the guide continually pointed out, the women didn't clutter their rooms with furniture: you could see exactly where the various pieces of furniture had stood in all the rooms, because around these empty spaces beautiful pictures had been painted, outlining the furniture. … And in the bedrooms the floors were covered with lovely mosaics, except for where the two beds had stood! They wanted nothing! —Rusty

"And the streets!" Rusty wrote:

Ruts worn deep where chariot after chariot had passed; the streets were lower than the house level, almost by a foot; and on the corners (or intersections!) there were three large stones … this was for the people to cross the street, so they would not have to step into the dirty, wet street (often filled with garbage … as they had no other place to put it sometimes). The three stones were so carefully placed that there was just exactly room for the chariot wheels to pass between them. And in the "business section:" of the city, the guide showed us that the families lived on the second floor, and on the first floor they had their "store." The front wall of all the stores was missing. … As the guide said, everyone could see them working hard. ... And if you wanted a copper kettle you went to the copper man and while he began to pound out the kettle, you stood and watched him, and you knew that he did not make it out of tin and cover it with copper ... like today!

 Also he said that the little boys playing in the streets had in their constant view these men working hard and honestly, and they grew up with the knowledge that they must work also and honestly! And the guide sagely continued "not like today, when the small boys play ball and play on the streets, out of sight of men making an honest living, and they grow up with the desire only to escape from work, and to have only a good time the rest of their lives."And he continued to philosophize and to compare the civilizations 2,000 years apart, for the remainder of the "visit."

We entered houses of rich men, of poor men, stores of pottery, stores of medicine, and the "Snack bars!" My goodness! Remember that the entire first floor of the building which was directly on the street had no 4ᵗʰ wall. ... And there was a bar (these snack bars were numerous in each block) ... all decorated in bright, gay mosaics; and behind were huge stone jugs and receptacles where they kept their food ... Some were near a small open stove to keep things hot. ... You had the feeling if you asked for a hot dog with mustard, it would suddenly appear. ... And the guide explained that the houses of the poorer people and the lower middle class could not afford to have a kitchen, and anyway cooking was very difficult then; so everyone ate at the snack bars, always standing ... never sitting. ... And we could just hear their conversations about the day, and their political arguments, and their rich laughter ... then we were shown many many baths ... public ... and some for all classes of people, each becoming more elaborate, but all were lovely and comfortable.

And for the richer, there were rooms upon rooms upon rooms, each serving a different purpose; some for undressing, some for sweating, some for swimming, some for scraping (servants scraped all the dead skin off), and some for oiling (servants also oiled all the people —- I don't mean servants, I mean slaves). The poor people had to scrape and oil themselves, but otherwise the same privileges were allowed them free ... And off the baths were "snack bars," and also places for the rich to dine ... but of course the rich could not stand while eating ... so there were huge stone "tables" at a slant ... usually two parallel to each other, with the higher ends facing each other, and in between was a round lower stone. ... The "tables" were for the men to lie on, and the round stone was for holding basins of water, into which the men could dip their sticky fingers ... the guide made Kit lie down "Roman" style while she "ate" and I took a picture. The guide was really a gem about pictures; he knew all the best angles for pictures, and exactly set for the time of the sun. ... We were terribly lucky because the sun began setting while we were there ... and the golden, rosy light reflecting on the columns and his lovely ghost of a city was a sight I can never forget and never cease to marvel at ... the last of our visit was paid to the Forum, where all the "banks," the political affairs, "lawyers," "doctors," etc., were located. ... And as the guide concluded there also, they were wiser than we; for example when a stranger came to the city, he knew exactly where he could to go to find exactly what he wanted, as this was the Roman plan for all cities. ... Now, he said, you must ask directions, and look at maps, and become thoroughly confused, and waste time, and lose patience, and get lost, and we agreed sooo heartily with him!! The Forum (as it must be in all Roman cities) was the most thrilling, the most stirring. ... Their ancient spirits were there – all around us – I felt awed and as if I

had suddenly stumbled in somewhere that I shouldn't be. ... I felt
an intruder – from another land and another era. ... And the setting
sun and the blue sky and rosy golden light reflected everywhere.

Kit in Pompeii.

[...] Also we saw the plaster covered bones [casts of bodies made
from volcanic ash] of some people who were caught in their homes or
shops or on the street ... there was a small boy whom they had
found crouched in a corner; and two other older boys (about 17, I
think) who had their arms around each other, clinging for protection
– So awful. Little did they dream that 2,000 years later they would
be discovered and gazed upon by people like themselves – Where
shall we be 2,000 years from now?

[...] Kit and I left Pompeii in a daze ... not speaking ... unwilling
to return to 1954 and to the noisy cars and buses ... we reached our
car and were besieged by a man and a girl who were selling
souvenirs and from whom it was almost impossible to get away!
They hung on us, and when I finally roared the engine and zoomed

away, they were flung back off the side of the car … Naples and the tourist venders! And we headed for Sorrento. —Rusty

That night, Rusty wrote a postcard to her mother:

Nov. 27, 1954

Sorrento

Dear Mom,

Pompei is unbelievable! We were here today from 2:30 till about 5:00 – This was their amphitheater – and planned so <u>perfectly</u>! The entrances and exits, etc. – are more clever than ours. – That is Vesuvius in the background, only she is not smoking now. In 1944 an eruption crumbled in the crater and the "hole" is all filled up; - actually much more dangerous, the guide said; so much may be gathering inside. …

The city is <u>160 square acres</u>, and is only 2/3rds excavated; - they are working on it further constantly –

Love,

Marialyce

After their trip to Pompeii, the girls drove on to Sorrento where they joined Dusty Rhodes, one of the American boys they'd met in Florence, for dinner and for the next few days in the Campania region of southern Italy. Although Kit never wrote a word about Pompeii in either her journal or her letters, she described the rest of the trip in more detail than Rusty.

Gorgeous day! We're in <u>heaven</u>. Beautiful sunshine, bright, bright blue sky – orange, palm and olive trees. Most fabulous wonderful feeling to be in a balmy sunny place the end of November. Two

Italian boys followed us for miles through Sorrento to our hotel! Stopped when we did and <u>insisted</u> on talking to us – Terribly funny – very Italian and persuasive in their way – Just can't be angry with them – Names of Nino and Tony (how Italian can you get?)

Beautiful beautiful hotel. Dusty is staying here (he recommended it). We're the only ones in the hotel. It is the [Hotel Pensione Minerva] on the outskirts of Sorrento – high up on a cliff overlooking Bay of Naples and Sorrento – We have a balcony! Warm, stars – wonderful air. Three of us ate dinner at Minervetta. Nino and friend appeared and we all went dancing in town. Good time. Going to Amalfi tomorrow. —Kit

The next day, Kit wrote:

Another perfect day. Bought another camera (Damn!) but glad I did – drove along the Amalfi drive – most beautiful scenery I've ever seen – winding road – high cliffs dropping sheer into bright blue and green Mediterranean. Three of us had a <u>marvelous</u> time. Dusty fits in just perfectly with us! Took multi pictures – couldn't begin to describe the perfect beauty of the day. Bought red wine, cheese and bread and stopped at a wonderful little grassy spot on the edge of a cliff for lunch – I don't <u>ever</u> want to leave.

Capri tomorrow – Oh, ate at [o'Perrucchiano] – <u>wonderful</u> – best food so far! Highly recommended. —Kit

In a postcard home, Rusty wrote about the day:

Nov. 28, 1954

Sorrento

Dearest Mom,

This is absolute <u>paradise</u>! Warm, palm trees, sunshine, aqua blue water – the <u>Mediterranean Sea</u>!!! And we <u>picked oranges</u> from the trees this afternoon and ate them!! Never have seen anything so beautiful!

We took the Amalfi Drive today and words just can't describe it. It's a road carved out of rock winding high on a cliff above the blue Mediterranean. I never want to leave!! We're going to Capri this morning – everything is happening and I just haven't had time to write – But will soon!

Love Marialyce

The girls and Dusty took the morning boat from Sorrento to Capri. Kit wrote, "Dashed madly to make morning boat – crazy

Dusty Rhodes and Rusty with a picnic lunch along the Amalfi coast.

run down millions of steps to the waterfront – little hotel man leading us all the way – got laughing so I couldn't run!" According to Kit's journal, both girls felt horrible at the end of the

35-minute ride. Fortunately, they recovered shortly after they docked.

Breakfast on our private terrace! - Dusty, Kit and waiter friend. Floridiana Capri. —Rusty

Hopped in hotel car (crazy things, they <u>all are</u> – old top down touring affair – loved it). Hotel [Floridiana] is marvelous – we each have double room with bath! Inexpensive (special price for us I think). Terrace with olive trees etc. all to ourselves – view of Mediterranean – absolutely the end! Paradise on earth is all I can say – I'll <u>never</u> forget it. —Kit

Although neither wrote about it (Kit only listed the destination in her journal), sometime during their second day on Capri, the girls visited Grotto Azzurra (the Blue Grotto), a natural sea cave with water the color of rich blues and greens. Later that day, Kit continued in her journal:

Still in heaven – nothing more to say – wandered all over today.
We're still getting on just wonderfully – a trio made in heaven for
paradise on earth! A bit flowery but true – watched the Tarantella
in the square tonight. Two adorable Italian boys (about 19 or 20)
followed us on our way to the john and begged us to go dancing
with them. They were simply darling and we would have loved to go
– but – we were tied up with Dusty and another fellow – soooo....
—Kit

The next morning, Kit, Rusty, and Dusty sat out on their terrace for a couple of hours relaxing in the warm sun. Kit wrote that life in Capri was "most perfect life in the world." The boat trip back to Sorrento was uneventful, but that night she and Dusty stayed up until 4:30 a.m. "He is much more of a Romeo than Rusty and I ever dreamed – Hmmmm!" She wrote, "We're all sorry to have to break up – Guess we'll never have such a wonderful, idyllic episode again."

32

Saying Arrivederci in Rome
(December 3 – December 16, 1954)

The drive back to Rome, was beautiful, warm, and sunny. Exhausted, Kit slept part of the way but woke when they ran out of gas on the highway. As the girls pushed Europa, Kit wrote, "Two Italians came along and tied the cars together with barbed wire! So we trundled merrily into the gas station!"

For the next several nights, the girls stayed with Signora Panico at 22 Via Reno in Rome. Kit wrote home that the place was "fabulous – only 750 lire including breakfast, heat, etc." Kit wrote about their hosts in her journal, "S. Panico and her son Berto are characters!" She described Signora Panico as blondish with a booming voice and Berto as "very Italian looking – dark – pixie-ish sense of humor."

Back in Rome, Kit and Rusty decided to find Sylvia, Alberto, and Rekin, the people who had helped them in the post office in November. At 6 p.m., they went to dinner at Taverna Margutta, the restaurant Alberto had recommended, but it was empty. When they bumped into Alberto the next day, he told them that no one ate as early as 6 p.m. They needed to go to dinner later. Eating a late dinner or even lunch at Taverna Margutta soon became routine. "That's how we met everyone," Rusty remembered years later. "That's where we had our meals."

Alberto took the girls to Café Greco, the oldest coffee house in Rome and then to lunch at Taverna Margutta where Rekin, who was from Turkey, joined them.

In Alberto's apartment, they drank a glass of bubbly wine called "Est! Est! Est!" Kit wrote that the apartment was "full of wonderful colorful abstracts." After dinner at "a marvelous pizza place called La Sacrestia (near Pantheon via Seminario)," the men took the girls for tartufo, "the best ice cream thing I've ever tasted" on the Piazzo Navona.

On Saturday, December 4, the girls read the newspaper on the Spanish Steps then accompanied Alberto and the others for lunch. In the afternoon, Rusty and Kit boarded an American Express bus for a tour of Rome. They visited the Basilica di Santa Maria Maggiore with its fifth century mosaics. They went to the Holy Steps, Scala Santa, which, according to tradition, were brought to Rome in the fourth century from Pontius Pilate's Palace in Jerusalem. They toured the Roman Coliseum. They were shown part of the ancient Appian Way and the underground Catacombs where early Christians had once been buried.

Through the excitement of their sightseeing and socializing, Rusty was apprehensive and scared. In only a few days, Kit would be leaving and she would be on her own. Rusty wrote to her mother on December 3:

A snapshot of some of the members of "the gang" in Rome.

Money – hate to mention it – but it's a very necessary evil; - and frankly I've been <u>scared</u> the last few days. – I have about $2.00 (two dollars) left, and then I start borrowing from Kit. … Was praying that some money would be at American Express from you when I came back to Rome from Capri. Am praying, though, that I will receive some money somehow in the next day or two. Kit doesn't have enough money left to support the two of us for very long. Her father sent her the $200.00 to restore her wardrobe after the theft but her boat ticket cost more than she had planned, and horrible, no ships are sailing from Italy in time to get her home for Christmas, - it's strange but true; - so she has to go back on the Mauretania (same line as Queen Mary) and consequently she has to sail from Le Havre, France! – So, plus her ticket on the ship, she had to buy an airplane ticket ($60.00) from Rome to Paris, and then she has to stay overnight in Paris – It really makes it all very complicated and not at all convenient!!! —Rusty

Her letter continues:

THANK YOU – for saying you are sending on some money for Christmas; - I didn't mean to sound ungrateful! – I am, more grateful than you know – But it's just that I have been going through all kinds of emotions during the last two weeks – one week in particular – of being honest-to-goodness right-down homesick; - of thinking I would give anything to be going home for Christmas, and suddenly being faced with the actual and rather overwhelming problem of "I have to find a job" – And where? I love Italy! I don't want to work in any other country, and yet, this is one of the most difficult – And my money is – no longer. As I said before, I'm scared – (to put it bluntly). However, today I feel much more optimistic! Rome is – the Best! Love it! And I'm staying at a pensione (private home) of the people with whom Cal lived when he was here 3 winters – They're wonderful – And I feel very good to know I have a place here! We must fly away now to have our first PIZZA in Italy! Will write more soon. —Rusty

Chris Willy along the Italian Riviera.

Only a few postcards were written after the girls arrived in Rome. Kit stopped writing letters home and in her journal. Rusty wrote in her letter home on December 3, "We are leaving Rome on Wednesday, December 8th, and are driving to the Riviera – (Italian, not French) for about 5 days. Plan to return to Rome on the 13th or 14th – Details later." But Rusty never did write about their trip to the Italian Riviera or their time together in Rome. According to Rusty's notes on her slides, the girls picnicked with Dusty Rhodes near Livorno on December 8 and visited the Leaning Tower of Pisa (not dated) before heading to Portofino where they spent the next five days. At some point, Dusty left, and Chris joined them, but according to Kit, the two men never met.

"We loved Portofino," Kit said in 2012. "The hotel we stayed at was marvelous. We were the only people staying in the hotel. I got very friendly with the owners and the people who worked there. We had a wonderful hike to San Fruttuoso. The hotel packed us a delicious lunch. When we were there, there were only five boats in the water. We hung out most of the day."

Rusty wrote her last postcard while with Kit on December 13 from Portofino on the Riviera:

Dec. 13, 1954

Portofino Riviera

Dearest Mom,

I'm sitting in the hot sunshine on a cliff overlooking the bluest blue Ligurian Sea! – Pine trees, cactus, palm trees and olive trees are above and around me – There's a lighthouse about 200 feet away – Heavenly!

Yesterday, we hiked 3 hours to the tiny village of Santa [San] Fruttuoso (this postcard) Fascinating – Description will follow in a letter – Watched fishermen pulling in their nets – Then took a boat back to our "home." Sun-bathing in December!

Lovingly,

Marialyce

Although neither wrote about their parting, Rusty and Kit often talked about it in later years. Kit said, "I remember we figured out how much money I would need on the trip home. I gave Marialyce $10."

At Ciampino, the Rome airport. Kit leaves me - and starts home. –Rusty

Rekin, their new Turkish friend, offered to accompany the girls to Rome's Ciampino Airport. According to Rusty, Rekin produced a Turkish radio show on which he gave news to Turks living in Rome. Tall and dark, Rusty said that he was "so sweet." As Kit walked toward the plane, "I turned around and started to walk back to the car," Rusty said. She remembered thinking, "Why is she leaving? She is so foolish," and then looked ahead at Europa and this dark, swarthy man. "I had $10 and one skirt I had borrowed from Kit and no place to live. I had nothing else. I thought, 'What am I doing?'"

Afterword

Rusty stayed in Italy for several months, continuing to write another 30 letters home to her mother. To make money, Rusty taught English (classes and private lessons) at Berlitz and found a few jobs dubbing Italian films. The friends she and Kit made

Rusty in Rome on her own.

became her family, Rekin Tokstoy and Haluk (Turkish); Harvey, Bill Kuehl, Sylvia, and Nadya Klotz (American); Queenie Tobakoff (South African), Nicky (English), and Alberto Arnoldi and Vincenzo Domina (Italian). She moved into an apartment on the Spanish Steps with Nadya at 176 Via Aurelia, Number 16, and began what soon turned into a serious romance with Vincenzo.

In June 1955, the letters stopped when Rusty's mother, Alice Tyler, arrived in Rome. Mother and daughter lived together while Rusty finished her teaching commitments, and on July 1, the two embarked on a trip around Europe. In August, Rusty wrote to Kit's parents:

> *How strange it seems to be back in Paris – in the summer and without Kit!! It's as lovely as ever, and yet I don't think it can ever be as beautiful as it was to us that week in September, really. It's fun, though, to be showing everything to Mom. … I'm surprised that I know my way around so well!*
>
> *Received three wonderful letters from Kit here. What a surprise to know that she's on her way to California now!! I think it's*

Rusty headed home on the Vulcania.

*marvelous! That's where I'd like to go next, too. … Maybe I will. … And she's going through South Dakota. … How I wish I was there to give her a real whirl around the prairie!! —*Rusty

Rusty sold Europa on August 18 in Nice for $685. From Nice, Rusty and Alice made their way south through Spain to Gibraltar, and in late August and early September, mother and daughter sailed back to the U.S. on the MS *Vulcania,* an Italian ocean liner. They slept in Room 513.

In New York City, they purchased a 1955 yellow Chevrolet for $1,599, which looked just like a New York City taxi cab. After a

Rusty's mother behind the wheel of the "taxi" they drove home to S. Dakota.

few days in New York, Rusty and Alice drove back to South Dakota, where Rusty worked as a child welfare worker for the State of South Dakota before moving to California.

Forty years later, in 1995, Rusty received a letter from Italy sent to "Marialyce Tyler, Fort Pierre, South Dakota." Although Rusty now lived in San Francisco, the post office in Fort Pierre knew her married name, Marialyce Dorward, and forwarded on the letter from Vincenzo. That letter is missing, but Rusty responded, and the two of them corresponded at Christmas time for another 10 or so years. Following are excerpts from Rusty's letter to Vincenzo, dated February 9, 1996, in which she summarizes her life.

Dear Vincenzo,

Italia still lives in my heart ... as do you. ... Simply amazing to hear from you after all these years. ...

Thank you for your sketch of 40 years. ... I am glad you are well and content. ...

Where to begin for me? This, too, will be only a sketch. ...

In April of 1956 I flew to San Francisco to attend Kit Tucker's wedding to Ross Cowan. Spending two weeks there, I knew this was where I wanted to live: moved here in 1957.

In September of 1959 I married Robert L. Abbott. We have three children: Tara Lynn ... Tane Robert ... and Kia Alice. We moved, just before Kia was born, from San Francisco across the Golden Gate Bridge to Marin County ... 3 years in Sausalito, and then to Belvedere. We had a lovely home on the Belvedere Lagoon, beside San Francisco Bay, looking across the Bay to the City.

My mother was married in 1963. She and my step-father built a lovely home in Fort Pierre; and I took my family back many times to visit. ...

Bob and I separated after 24 years of marriage, divorcing 7 ½ years later. From 1980 I had been acting professionally, making a few TV commercials, tiny parts in movies, big part in one TV show, etc. But after Bob and I separated, I began working full time as a real estate agent, selling and listing homes in Marin County.

My youngest child, Kia, was married in July of 1989. I am enclosing a picture that was taken at her wedding. Tara is on the left, then Kia, her new husband Paul Graham Ray, myself, and my son Tane. Both Tane and Kia have red hair. ... Tane's eyes are brown, Kia's are green. Tara is a blue-eyed blonde. They are wonderful people, and I adore them. ...

In 1990, I met Dave Dorward, a truly wonderful man. ... Dave and I were married on the 4th of July, 1991. In 1993 Dave and I moved from Belvedere to San Rafael, still in Marin County, just further north. Dave retired from his company, Cagwin & Dorward Landscape Contractors, at the end of 1994. I retired from working for Coldwell Banker Real Estate in February, 1995. ...

Though I have travelled a good deal over the years. ... I've been to Greece, London, Turkey, French Riviera, Panama, Canada, Mexico, Hawaii, Thailand, Malaysia, Singapore, Hong Kong. ... I have never returned to Italy. I really want to and yet in 40 years I know things have changed ... and in some ways I don't want to see the changes. ... It was a wonderful time of my life, and I am grateful that I was there at a perfect time. I have dear friends who keep saying they want Dave and me to go to Italy with them ... and though it will probably be two years before we can, I think probably we will. I need to take some classes in Italian (my vocabulary is hidden deep in my mind). On February 25th, we leave for 2 weeks to Egypt, where I've wanted to visit since I was a child.

Nadya and Valerio are still married and live in Carmel, California. I have seen them on and off over the years quite a bit. They have two daughters ... both now married and living nearby.

I saw Bill Kuehl once in New York in January, 1980. ...

At various times over earlier years I've seen "Butch," Victor with his daughter Ruth, and some others whom I can't even remember now.

In 1977 in Istanbul I tried to find Rekin Tokstoy. Found that name in the phone book, called several times, there was not answer. Then I wrote a letter to the address listed, but it was returned to me.

Those days in Rome are all so vivid to me. Almost impossible to realize it has been over 40 years. How can that be?

With affection,

Marialyce

P.S. I misplaced your address, that is why this letter has taken so long! I am glad you wrote again!

Sometime around 2009, Marialyce (aka Rusty) stopped hearing from Vincenzo. She passed away on May 22, 2012, at the age of 82. She never visited Rome again.

Postcard from Kit to Rusty:

December 16, 1954

Hello —

Gee, it's great traveling by plane! It only took us 10 1/2 hours to get to Paris! I have just arrived at the station and am standing here waiting for Chris' train. We got bumped off the plane at Lyon because Paris and surrounding territory for hundreds of miles around was closed in by fog! Spent five hours on the train – I'm dead! Flew up to Nice on same plane with Errol Flynn! He wouldn't speak to me - ! Are you okay? Please take care -! Guess what – I'm in Paris again!

Love, Kit

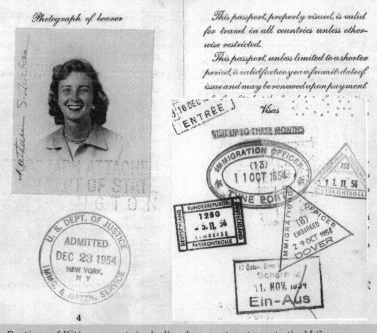

Portions of Kit's passport, including her reentry stamp to the U.S.

After two days in Paris with their British friend Chris Willy, Kit sailed home on the RMS *Mauretania* with their American friend Dusty Rhodes. She said that it was very, very difficult to leave Europe. "I would have loved to have stayed. We [Kit and Rusty] were so close." Seasick and sad, Kit said she didn't think she could have survived the trip home without Dusty. "It was ghastly," she said.

Home in time for Christmas, Kit hunkered down with family, before returning to her job at NBC. Dusty lived in Pennsylvania and the two of them dated for several months. Kit received the following letter from Rekin some time that winter:

Rome, 18. L. 1955

Dear Kit,

For the first time in my life, I am writing a letter in English. I am asking myself, how I found the courage of write in a linguage that even I can't speak. (You saw, how poor was, the English of all of us.) But your pictures that Marialyce refused to send you, telling me "Why don't you send yourself," obliged me to try that.

From your letters to Marialyce, we learned that you had a good trip. We had been glad, to learn also, that you were sorry to left Rome. Because we hope to see you again here, with us. The day of your departure, you promised a cup of coffee to Marialyce and we, at the airport. We are still waiting for our coffees. But I am sure that we'll have them, before the end of the opera season.

I wish to write you a long letter. But you must understand, how it's difficult for me. I wrote this letter in a week. For a long one, I must spend at least a month. So I prefer to cut here.

I hope to see you again soon, and send you all my regards and my best wishes.

Rekin Tokstoy

In August, Kit took another leave of absence from NBC and flew to San Francisco to spend time with her sister who was having a baby. "I fell in love with San Francisco, and my old job didn't seem all that fun anymore. I wrote back to New York and resigned." Kit found work through a temp agency, and in October she found a room at Chateau Bleu, a boarding house in San Francisco.

She met her future husband, Ross Cowan, in Chateau Bleu's dining room. "He [Ross] needed a date to visit some friends who were going out to dinner so he took me," Kit said. "I remember sitting at the bar and talking, and we discovered that we both had read Christopher Robin, and we both liked ballet." The two married and lived in the San Francisco Bay Area for a few years

Kit and Ross Cowan -- Engaged.

where their first son, Christopher Tucker Cowan, was born in 1956.

Over the next 40 years, the couple raised a family in Denver, Colorado; New Brunswick and Morristown, New Jersey; and Concord, Massachusetts while Ross moved around in the business world of reinsurance. Andrew Joseph was born in New Brunswick in 1960, and Nancy Anne was born in Morristown in 1965.

Kit went to work for Ross when he started his own business, RC Cowan Insurance Company, in Hartford, Connecticut. At that time they lived in Madison, Connecticut. In 1994, Kit and Ross retired and transferred their residence to Oak Bluffs, Massachusetts, a town on Martha's Vineyard.

Ross had never been abroad, so Kit said she led him around in 1971 for three weeks. "We spent one week in London, one week in Paris, and one week in Rome." They continued to travel over the years, returning several times to England and to Italy. On one visit, Kit took Ross to San Fruttuoso where they stayed at the same hotel that Kit and Rusty visited years before. In 1998, they took a trip with friends, sailing off the southwest coast of Turkey for 10 days. In 2012, they toured Ireland for the first time.

Currently, Kit and Ross spend the warm months at their home on Martha's Vineyard, where they enjoy gardening, sailing, and golf. They also have an apartment in Boston's Back Bay where they take in the symphony, visit museums, and spend time with their grandchildren.

Kit (on left) and Rusty on the Vineyard in 2005.

Kit and Rusty remained close friends, though they lived 3,000 miles apart. Rusty said that Kit was the sister she never had. Throughout the years, they wrote letters and visited each other in Massachusetts and in California. Whenever they were together, they often reminisced about their unique experiences, and the many special people they met, on their Tucker - Tyler Adventure.

Acknowledgments

Thanks to Rusty and Kit and their parents for saving all those letters and slides, without which this book would have been impossible. Thank you for sharing with us your letters as well as your journal, Kit, and for answering our never-ending questions.

Adventures would not be possible without the support and camaraderie of friends and family. Thank you to Rusty's friend and roommate in college and in New York, Eve Johnson, for clarifying details of their time together and for sharing with us her letters from Rusty.

Thanks to Tara's aunt, Sharon Cusick, who read and edited in great detail the drafts of our book and to Tara's father, Robert Abbott, and his partner, Gloria Heidi, for their words of wisdom and support along the way.

Thank you Jennifer Miller, Sarah Skoletsky, Nancy Shohet West, and Donna Woelki who read drafts of this book and offered constructive criticism and positive feedback; to Betsy Stepp for her creative use of many elements to design the cover and maps; and to the Concord Public Library and Nashoba Brook Bakery for giving us a place to work and collaborate.

A special thank you to our families, who listened to various quotes, viewed the slides, humored us as we spoke with enthusiasm and excitement, and gave us the time and space we needed to achieve our goal. This book is for you and the generations after you.

—Nancy and Tara

Notes to the Reader

As we read through and edited the many letters and journal pages of The Tucker ~ Tyler Adventure, our goal was to create an engaging travelogue of Kit's and Rusty's three months together. As editors, we made a few assumptions and editorial decisions.

In many cases, the two women described the same event or place. We chose what we thought were the best descriptions and interpretations of the trip. Rusty and Kit wrote with such flourish and personality, we hesitated to make any changes or corrections unless we felt that punctuation or misspellings would hinder the reader. Rusty's letters are filled with ellipses and dashes. Kit's letters include the occasional slang or colorful anecdote. Both Rusty and Kit scattered exclamation marks liberally throughout their letters. In general, punctuation was left as is, errors and all.

Because Rusty wrote detailed descriptions on each slide, captions for most of the photographs were written by Rusty and obtained from the slides on which they were written. The traveled route, as shown on the maps, was estimated based on their letters and likely driving routes found by using Google Maps.

All personal communication used as references, including letters, journals, postcards, and interviews, is detailed below by chapter. All correspondence from Kit and Rusty was written to their families unless otherwise noted.

Chapter 1: Meeting the Girls

Information on the background of Katherine Tucker was obtained through personal communication with the authors in 2005, 2011, 2012, and 2013. Information on the background of Marialyce Tyler was obtained through personal communication in 2005 and 2007 and with Evelyn Luft Johnson via telephone and e-mail in 2010, 2012, and 2013. Additional information was obtained from letters Marialyce Tyler wrote to Evelyn Luft, dated January 11 and 31, and April 17, 1953, and to Cal Johnson, dated August 4, 1954, and from notes written by Marialyce Tyler on her slides.

Chapter 2: Sailing to Europe

Information and excerpts were obtained from the following: personal communication with Katherine Cowan and Marialyce Dorward in 2005; entries by Katherine Tucker's journal dated September 8, September 9, September 10, September 11, September 12, and September 13, 1954; a letter from Katherine Tucker dated September 8-9, 1954; and letters from Marialyce Tyler to her mother dated September 8-9, September 14, September 15, and September 16, 1954.

Chapter 3: Taking the Train Through Normandy

Information and excerpts were obtained from the following: personal communication with Katherine Cowan in 2011; entries from Katherine Tucker's journal dated September 13, 1954; a letter from Katherine Tucker dated September 16, 1954; a letter from Marialyce Tyler to Cal Johnson dated August 4, 1954 and to her mother dated September 17, 1954; and a postcard dated September 19, 1954.

Chapter 4: Discovering Paris

Information and excerpts were obtained from the following: entries by Katherine Tucker's journal dated September 14 and September 18, 1954; a letter from Katherine Tucker dated September 16, 1954; and letters from Marialyce Tyler entitled,

"The Paris Edition, Chapter 1," dated September 22, 1954 and another letter entitled, "The Paris Edition, Chapter 3," undated.

Chapter 5: Exploring the Left Bank and the Latin Quarter

Information and excerpts were obtained from the following: entries from Katherine Tucker's journal dated September 16 and 17, 1954; a letter from Katherine Tucker dated September 16, 1954; and letters from Marialyce Tyler entitled, "The Paris Edition, Chapter 2," undated, and "The Paris Edition, Chapter 3," undated.

Chapter 6: Picking Up a Car in Paris

Information and excerpts were obtained from the following: entries from Katherine Tucker's journal dated September 15 and 17, 1954, and a letter from Marialyce Tyler entitled, "The Paris Edition, Last Chapter – Paris – No. 4," and undated.

Chapter 7: Viewing Versailles

Information and excerpts were obtained from the following: entries from Katherine Tucker's journal dated September 19 and 20, 1954; a letter from Katherine Tucker dated September 19, 1954; and a letter from Marialyce Tyler dated September 19, 1954.

Chapter 8: Smuggling in and out of Belgium

Information and excerpts were obtained from the following: entries from Katherine Tucker's journal dated September 21 and 22, 1954; a letter from Katherine Tucker dated September 22, 1954, and a letter from Marialyce Tyler dated September 24, 1954.

Chapter 9: Hearing Rubinstein in Holland

Information and excerpts were obtained from the following: entries from Katherine Tucker's journal dated September 23, September 24, September 25, September 26, and September 27,

1954; a letter from Katherine Tucker dated September 23 and 29, 1954, and a letter from Marialyce Tyler dated September 29, 1954.

Chapter 10: Glimpsing Germany

Information and excerpts were obtained from the following: entries from Katherine Tucker's journal dated September 28, 1954; letters from Katherine Tucker dated September 23 and 29, 1954; and a letter from Marialyce Tyler dated September 29, 1954.

Chapter 11: Dining in Denmark

Information and excerpts were obtained from the following: entries from Katherine Tucker's journal dated September 29, September 30, October 1, and October 2, 1954; letters from Katherine Tucker dated September 29, October 2, October 4, and October 7, 1954; and letters from Marialyce Tyler dated October 4, October 5, October 6, October 7, 1954.

Chapter 12: Touring Through Sweden

Information and excerpts were obtained from the following: entries from Katherine Tucker's journal dated October 2, October 3, and October 4, 1954; a postcard from Katherine Tucker dated October 7, 1954; and a letter from Marialyce Tyler dated October 7, 1954.

Chapter 13: Cascading in Norway

Information and excerpts were obtained from the following: personal communication with Katherine Cowan on June 26, 2013; entries from Katherine Tucker's journal dated October 4, October 5, October 6, October 7, October 8, and October 9, 1954; a letter from Katherine Tucker dated October 14, 1954; postcards from Katherine Tucker dated October 7 and October 13, 1954; and letters from Marialyce Tyler dated October 7, October 8, and

October 13, 1954.

Chapter 14: Climbing Castles in Scotland

Information and excerpts were obtained from the following: entries from Katherine Tucker's journal dated October 11, October 12, October 13, and October 14, 1954; letters from Katherine Tucker dated October 14 and October 18, 1954; a postcard from Katherine Tucker dated October 13, 1954; and letters from Marialyce Tyler dated October 13, October 14 and October 18, 1954.

Chapter 15: Shattering a Window in Northwest England

Information and excerpts were obtained from the following: entries from Katherine Tucker's journal dated October 15 and October 16, 1954, and letters from Marialyce Tyler dated October 15 and October 18, 1954.

Chapter 16: Rubbernecking in London

Information and excerpts were obtained from the following: entries from Katherine Tucker's journal dated October 18, October 19, and October 20, 1954; a letter from Katherine Tucker dated October 6 and October 30, 1954; and letters from Marialyce Tyler dated October 16, October 24, and October 29, 1954.

Chapter 17: Sipping Sherry in Oxford and Tea in London

Information and excerpts were obtained from the following: personal communication with Marialyce Dorward in 2007; entries from Katherine Tucker's journal dated October 21, October 22, October 23, October 24, October 25, and October 26, 1954; letters from Katherine Tucker dated October 30 and November 4; letters from Marialyce Tyler dated November 2, November 3, and December 12, 1954; and a postcard dated October 16, 1954.

Chapter 18: Taking in the Theater in Stratford-Upon-Avon

Information and excerpts from letters were obtained from the following: entries from Katherine Tucker's journal dated October 27-28, 1954; and a postcard from Marialyce Tyler dated October 27, 1954.

Chapter 19: Crossing the English Channel

Information and excerpts from letters were obtained from the following: entries from Katherine Tucker's journal dated October 28 and October 29, 1954; a letter from Katherine Tucker dated November 3, 1954; and letters from Marialyce Tyler dated October 28, November 3, and November 4, 1954.

Chapter 20: Returning to Paris

Information and excerpts from letters were obtained from the following: entries from Katherine Tucker's journal dated October 29, October 30, November 1, and November 2, 1954; a letter from Katherine Tucker dated November 4, 1954; and letters from Marialyce Tyler dated November 4, November 11 (Munich), November 11 (Innsbruck), November 12, 1954; and a postcard from Marialyce Tyler dated November 2, 1954.

Chapter 21: Losing Possessions in Luxembourg

Information and excerpts from letters were from the following: entries from Katherine Tucker's journal dated November 3, 1954; a letter from Katherine Tucker dated November 3, 1954; and a letter from Marialyce Tyler dated November 4, 1954.

Chapter 22: Clinking in Germany

Information and excerpts from letters were obtained from the following: personal communication with Marialyce Dorward in

2007; entries from Katherine Tucker's journal dated November 5, November 6, November 7, November 8, November 9, November 10, and November 11, 1954; letters from Marialyce Tyler dated November 11 (Munich), November 13, November 14, and November 15, 1954.

Chapter 23: Clambering in Austria

Information and excerpts were obtained from the following: entries from Katherine Tucker's journal dated November 11, November 12, and November 13, 1954; and a letter from Marialyce Tyler dated November 15, 1954.

Chapter 24: Lingering in Lucerne

Information and excerpts were obtained from the following: entries from Katherine Tucker's journal dated November 13, November 14, November 15, November 16, and 17, 1954; and letters from Marialyce Tyler dated November 15 and November 20, 1954.

Chapter 25: Learning the Language in Italy

Information and excerpts were obtained from the following: entries from Katherine Tucker's journal dated November 18, 1954; a letter from Katherine Tucker dated November 18, 1954; and a letter from Marialyce Tyler dated December 17, 1954.

Chapter 26: Sightseeing in Milan

Information and excerpts were obtained from the following: entries from Katherine Tucker's journal dated November 19, 1954; a letter from Katherine Tucker dated November 18, 1954; and a letter from Marialyce Tyler dated December 17, 1954.

Chapter 27: Punting in Verona and Venice

Information and excerpts were obtained from the following: entries from Katherine Tucker's journal dated November 20, November 21, and November 22, 1954; a letter from Katherine Tucker dated November 18, 1954; a postcard from Marialyce dated November 20, 1954; and letters from Marialyce Tyler dated December 17, 1954, February 14, 1955, and February 25, 1955.

Chapter 28: Shopping in Florence

Information and excerpts were obtained from the following: entries from Katherine Tucker's journal dated November 22, November 23, and November 24, 1954; and letters from Marialyce Tyler dated February 25 and 26, 1955, and April 26, 1955.

Chapter 29: Feasting in Italy

Information and excerpts were obtained from the following: entries from Katherine Tucker's journal dated November 25, 1954; a letter from Marialyce Tyler dated November 25, 1954.

Chapter 30: Celebrity Gazing in Rome

Information and excerpts were obtained from the following: entries from Katherine Tucker's journal dated November 26, 1954; letters from Marialyce Tyler dated March 12, 1955.

Chapter 31: Sunning on the Amalfi Coast

Information and excerpts were obtained from the following: entries from Katherine Tucker's journal dated November 27, November 28, November 29, November 30, December 1, and December 2, 1954; postcards from Marialyce dated November 27 and 28, 1954; and letters from Marialyce Tyler dated March 12, May 17, and May 18, 1955.

Chapter 32: Saying Arrivederci in Rome

Information and excerpts were obtained from the following: personal communication with Katherine Cowan and Marialyce Dorward in 2005, 2007, and 2012; entries from Katherine Tucker's journal dated December 3 and December 4, 1954; postcards from Marialyce dated December 13, 1954; letters from Marialyce Tyler dated December 3, 1954; and an interview with Katherine Tucker Cowan dated December 12, 2012.

Afterword

Information and excerpts were obtained from the following: personal communication with Katherine Cowan in 2012 and Marialyce Dorward in 2007; letters from Marialyce Tyler to Mr. and Mrs. Tucker dated August 10, 1955; from Rekin Tokstoy to Katherine Tucker in 1955; and from Marialyce Tyler Dorward to Vincenzo Domina February 9, 1996. Information on Rusty's trip home, the sale of the Renault, and the purchase of the Chevrolet was obtained from the journal of Alice Tyler, dated July and August 1955.

Bibliography

American Memory of the 1950s Housewife. "Stereotypes." Accessed May 2013. http://americanmemoryofthe1950shousewif.bgsu.wikispaces.net/Stereotypes.

An American in Paris. DVD. directed by Vincente Minnelli. 1951; Burbank, CA: Warner Home Video. 2000.

Bach Cantatas. "Anna McKnight = Anna de Cavalieri (Soprano)." Accessed May 2013. http://www.bach-cantatas.com/Bio/McKnight-Anne.htm.

Bobborst.com. "Billboard Top 30 Songs of 1954 – Year-End Charts." Accessed December 11, 2013. http://www.bobborst.com/popculture/top-100-songs-of-the-year/?year=1954.

BootsnAll Travel Network. "All Saints' Day in France." Accessed June 11, 2013. http://www.francetravelguide.com/all-saints-day-in-france.html.

Brown, Betsy. "Seeking Our Fortunes." *House Beautiful*. October 1999.

Cowan, Katherine. Notes to Tara Taft. September 2011.

Cowan, Katherine. Personal interview with Nancy Cowan. 2011.

Cowan, Katherine. Personal interviews with Tara Taft. May 2005 and December 12, 2012.

Cowan, Katherine. Personal interview with Nancy Cowan and Tara Taft, June 26, 2013.

Dorward, Marialyce. Letter to Vincenzo Domina. February 9, 1996.

Dorward, Marialyce. Personal interviews with Tara Taft. May 2005 and December 2007.

Dunning, John. *On the Air, the Encyclopedia of Old Time Radio*. Oxford: Oxford University Press. 1998.

Dunford, Martin. *The Rough Guide to Rome*. New York: Rough Guides. 2012.

Encyclopedia Brittanica. "Simplon Tunnel." Accessed May 2013. http://www.britannica.com/EBchecked/topic/545413/Simplon-Tunnel

Fodor's. *Fodor's Rome: with the Best City Walks and Scenic Day Trips*. New York: Fodor's Travel. 2012.

Fodor's. *Fodor's The Amalfi Coast, Capri & Naples*. New York: Fodor's Travel. 2011.

Frame, Chris. *Chris' Cunard Page*. E-mail correspondence to Tara Taft. July 28, 2013.

Halliburton, Richard. *Richard Halliburton's Complete Book of Marvels*. Indianapolis: The Bobbs-Merrill Company, Inc. 1960.

Hart, Jeffrey Peter. *When the Going Was Good!: American Life in the Fifties*. New York: Jeffrey Hart Crown Publishers, Inc. 1982.

Harvard Student Agencies, Inc. *Let's Go Western Europe: The Student Travel Guide*. Cambridge: Let's Go, Inc. 2010.

History.com. "This Day in History. May 5, 1955: Allies End Occupation of West Germany." Accessed May 5, 2013. http://www.history.com/this-day-in-history/allies-end-occupation-of-west-germany.

Homes.com. "40 W. 74th Street. #2, New York." Property Details. http://www.homes.com/property/40-w-74th-st-new-york-ny-10023/id-400020531393/.

IMDb. *Apache*. Accessed June 7, 2013. http://www.imdb.com/title/tt0046719/.

IMDb. *The Green Scarf*. Accessed June 7, 2013. http://www.imdb.com/title/tt0047051/?ref_=fn_al_tt_1.

IMDb. *The Red Shoes*. Accessed June 2, 2013. http://www.imdb.com/title/tt0040725/.

IMDb. *Susan Slept Here*. Accessed June 7, 2013. http://www.imdb.com/find?q=susan+slept+here&s=all.

IMDb. *Three Steps to Heaven*. Accessed June 2, 2013. http://www.imdb.com/title/tt0045446/combined.

IMDb. *The Young Lovers*. Accessed June 7, 2013. http://www.imdb.com/title/tt0046846/?ref_=fn_al_tt_1.

Johnson, Evelyn. E-mail message to Tara Taft. February 2, 2012.

Johnson, Evelyn. Personal communication with Tara Taft. 2010, 2012, and 2013.

Jorgensen, Steffen Elmer. "A Ferry Tale for Motorists." Heritage Agency of Denmark. Accessed December 12, 2013. http://www.kulturarv.dk/1001fortaellinger/en_GB/halsskov-knudshoved-ferry-harbour/images.

KC Library Lonestar College. "American Cultural History. 1950-1959." Accessed May 2013. http://kclibrary.lonestar.edu/decade50.html.

Michelin & Cie. "Simplon Tunnel." Michelin & Cie. Accessed May 2013. http://www.isyours.com/e/guide/valais/simplon.html.

Mike's Engineering Wonders: Vintage Pages from the 1930s. "Alpine Tunnels."
Accessed May 2013. http://www.engwonders.byethost9.com/e079.html.

NADA Guides. 1955 Renault 4CV 4 Door Sedan Values. Accessed December 8,
2013. http://www.nadaguides.com/Classic-Cars/1955/Renault/4CV/4-Door-
Sedan/Values.

NBC.com. "The Tonight Show Experience: Steve Allen Bio." Accessed May 27,
2013. http://www.nbc.com/the-tonight-show-experience/hosts/steve-allen.shtml.

NPG. "NPG Facts and Figures: Historical Population Growth." Accessed May 5,
2013. http://www.npg.org/facts/us_historical_pops.htm.

PBS.org. "People & Events: Mrs. America: Women's Roles in the 1950s."
Accessed May 2013.
http://www.pbs.org/wgbh/amex/pill/peopleevents/p_mrs.html.

The People History. "The Year 1954 From the People History." Accessed June 12,
2013. http://www.thepeoplehistory.com/1954.html.

Pollak, Michael. "Answers to Questions About New York: West Side Roundup."
New York Times, January 6, 2013.

"Programme for To-Day." September 12, 1954.

Queenmary.com. "Ship Statistics and Details." Accessed May 2013.
http://www.queenmary.com/our-story/comparison.php.

Roman Holiday. DVD. Directed by William Wyler. 1953; Los Angeles, CA:
Paramount. 2002.

Sabrina. DVD. Directed by Billy Wilder. 1954; Los Angeles, CA: Paramount. 2001.

State of New Jersey Department of Labor Workforce and Development. "Table 6:
New Jersey Resident Population by Municipality 1930-1990." Accessed May 27,
2013. www.lwd.dol.state.nj.us/laborlpa/census/1990/poptrd6.html.

Stoneham, Nina. "Women's Roles in the 1950s." *1950sweebly.com*. Accessed May
2013. http://1950s.weebly.com/womens-roles.html.

Three Coins in the Fountain. DVD. Directed by Jean Negulesco. 1954; Los Angeles,
CA: 20th Century Fox. 2004.

Tokstoy, Rekin. Letter to Katherine Tucker. 1955. Rome, Italy

Triomfdervrede. "The Peace Palace, Temple of Peace, and Law." Accessed May
27, 2013.
http://www.triomfdervrede.nl/index.php?option=com_content&view=article&id
=17&Itemid=19&lang=en.

Tucker, Katherine. Collection of letters and postcards to family dated September 8 to November 18, 1954.

Tucker, Katherine. Journal. Entries dated September 8 - December 4, 1954.

Tyler, Alice. Journal. Entries dated August 18 and September 3, 1955.

Tyler, Marialyce. Collection of letters and postcards to Alice Tyler. September 8, 1954 to May 18, 1955.

Tyler, Marialyce. Letter to Cal Johnson. August 4, 1954. Fort Pierre, South Dakota.

Tyler, Marialyce. Letters to Evelyn Luft. January 11, January 31, and April 17, 1953. New York, New York.

Tyler, Marialyce. Letter to Mr. and Mrs. Tucker. August 10, 1955.

Tyler. Marialyce. Resume. Undated.

The Walks of Italy Blog. "Attending Opera in the Arena of Verona." Accessed May 2013. http://www.walksofitaly.com/blog/venice/attending-opera-in-the-arena-of-verona.

Wikipedia. "Milan-Domodossola Railway." Accessed May 2013. https://en.wikipedia.org/wiki/Milan–Domodossola_railway.

About the Authors

Tara Taft inherited her mother's sense of adventure and wanderlust. She loves to share stories and photos of her travels on her blog, snapshotsandsojourns.com. When she's not traveling, she lives with Sandy, Tommy, Erica, and their dog, Tilly, in Stow, Massachusetts.

Nancy Cowan lives with her family (Nathan, Katherine, Samantha, Spencer, and Zyler) in Carlisle, Massachusetts. She has traveled to many of the same places her mother did, but does not think she would ever be brave enough to share her journals with her daughters.

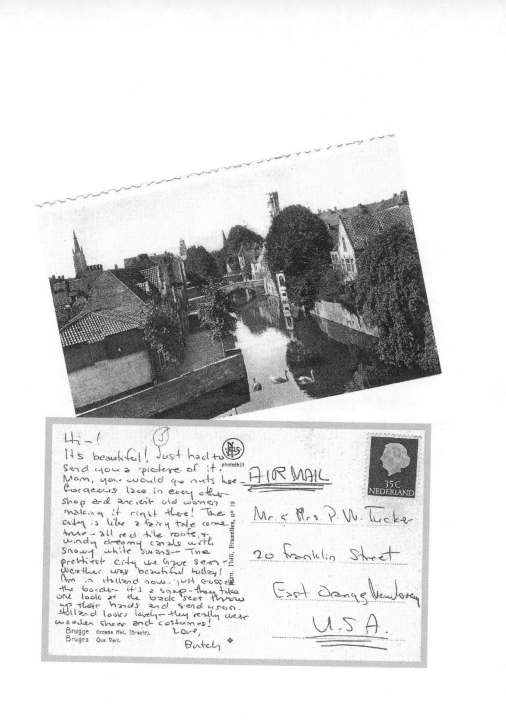

Hi -!

It's beautiful! Just had to send you a picture of it. Mom, you would go nuts here - Gorgeous lace in every other shop and ancient old women making it right there! The city is like a fairy tale come true - all red tile roofs, & windy dreamy canals with snowy white swans - The prettiest city we have seen - Weather was beautiful today! I'm in Holland now - just crossed the border - it's a snap - they take one look at the back seat throw up their hands and send us on. Holland looks lovely - they really wear wooden shoes and costumes!

Love,

Butch

Brugge Groene Rei. (Gracht).
Bruges Quai Vert.

AIR MAIL

35C NEDERLAND

Mr. & Mrs. P. W. Tucker

20 Franklin Street

East Orange New Jersey

U.S.A.